ALL GENERATIONS

A Handbook for Leaders of Family Worship

by

THE OFFCHURCH GROUP

CIO PUBLISHING
Church House, Dean's Yard, London SW1P 3NZ

ISBN 0 7151 0388 1

Published for the General Synod Board of Education
by the Church Information Office

Printed in England by Page Bros (Norwich) Ltd

CONTENTS

FOREWORD

The use of the word 'family' to describe acts of worship is widespread and growing. Its use is puzzling since it is often not at all clear precisely what it means and one wonders sometimes if it would make any difference at all to the style and content of worship if the adjective were dropped.

'What is family worship?' therefore is a pressing question and one of the great merits of this book is that it does not sit in judgment on the various kinds of worship labelled 'family' but, accepting the diversity, tries to give some content to the use of such a label. My experience is that the main intention in using this adjective is to bring all ages into a common worshipping experience. Family worship should not be worship for adults with some attention given to the presence of children, or worship really designed for children with an attempt made to make it tolerable for parents. It should be the provision of worship for the whole Christian community with all its diversity of age and experience; an integrated activity.

We are realising more and more that some of the difficulties we encounter in Christian growth are due to the separation of children from the worshipping community. Of course we worship God because he is worthy to be worshipped and not for any 'spin-off' such activity may bring. Worship is an end in itself. Yet it would be foolish not to recognise that the experience of worship is a crucial factor in Christian growth. While we do not worship God in order to grow, nevertheless if our experience of worship is deficient, then our growth is stunted. The worshipping community is the proper context for Christian nurture and if we fail to initiate the children into the fullness of worship, we ought not to be surprised if they in turn are not satisfied with their diet. We lose more people through spiritual malnutrition than we realise.

I commend this book therefore because it is a serious attempt to explore what 'family', 'all-age', 'integrated' worship really means. In addition to that it is practical and down to earth, full of information and rich in suggestion, and is therefore an invaluable resource book for all who have responsibilities for the ordering of worship.

May it deepen understanding and enlarge our experience of Christian worship.   + JOHN COVENTRY

A FREE CHURCH COMMENT

Within the Free Church tradition the adjective 'Free' implies amongst other things a principle of freedom in worship. This has not always been appreciated, nor have the unique opportunities afforded by this freedom always been seized by ministers and people. These are times of questioning and appraisal, and it is a matter of some urgency that the Free Churches should scrutinise their services of worship carefully, both in the inherited patterns and also in the many *ad hoc* 'happenings' that are being tried under the name of family worship. This book will be very helpful in this respect.

Part One speaks about family worship in its setting and includes much that is already within the tradition of the Free Churches. I envisage much fruitful discussion and planning taking place by groups of elders, deacons or chapel stewards who are prepared to discuss the life and worship of their church in the light of what is said here. The material could well provide an agenda for a series of meetings or house groups with a view to some action being taken in the church. For instance, the remarks made about the position of children in church should help those churches still wrestling with the problem of the status of children within the membership. The question of children at Communion is raised in Part Three. The Free Churches are having to debate this question as more and more parents are seeking some form of family spirituality which can find its inspiration in the family at Communion. The documents referred to in this section need to be studied by the Free Churches as the debate continues.

Having agreed in principle that some renewal in worship might happen, those who plan and lead will find the practical approach in Parts Two and Three very helpful. One of the problems which leaders have to face is finding a correct balance between the various elements which go to make up a satisfactory worship pattern. The original Free Church protest in worship led to an over-emphasis on the Bible and preaching; reaction to this has led some to a rejection of the sermon altogether and its replacement with other things. Leaders of Free Church worship could well look at their own patterns of service in the light of the various suggestions made in Part Two in which due attention is paid to finding a suitable mix of the various ingredients of worship.

Free Churchmen will probably find difficulty in assimilating some of the points made in Part Three, particularly where the Anglican authors are talking about the 'celebrant' at the Eucharist ('celebrant' is not a Free Church word). Nevertheless, the basic premise that those responsible for leading worship round the Table should look with some care at their actions holds good for us too.

Many Free Churches, as no doubt many Anglican churches, are experiencing great difficulty in trying to adapt their churches for different styles of worship. So many Free Church chapels were designed for speaking and listening only; dominated by pews and pulpit and organ, they are not suited to the more flexible forms of church services. The problems are by no means solved in this book, but they are highlighted in Part Three and the suggestions made would merit careful attention by any church meeting which wants to review its worship situation, particularly if new building or adaptation of existing premises is envisaged.

In their section on ideas and themes for worship (Part Four) the authors might be accused of allowing experience and psychology to dictate too readily to tradition and liturgy. On the other hand, what Minister or leader of family worship does not welcome ideas for the Family Service! These ideas are not intended to be chains, nor are they a comprehensive programme of sermon suggestions, but they should set you thinking about how your family worship can be geared towards involving more people as well as exciting your imagination to produce ideas of your own.

I should like to commend this book to our Free Churches as a useful aid to any leaders of congregations who want to stimulate their people to look carefully and constructively at their corporate life of worship. It should prove to be a handy resource book for Ministers, lay preachers and leaders of worship who are at present discussing this vital and privileged task of renewal in worship.

DAVID TENNANT

Westhill College of Education   Tutor in Christian Education
1979

HOW TO USE THIS BOOK

We are attempting, broadly speaking, a two-fold task in this book: first, to explore and understand the significance of church worship in which people of all ages are taking part; and second, to provide a substantial resource-book of ideas, suggestions and practical advice for clergy and lay people who are responsible for the ordering of family services.

The title of the book is therefore of some importance in suggesting how it should be used. The words 'All generations shall call me blessed' from the Magnificat are expressive of the prime reason for worship, namely, the human response to the God who created heaven and earth and showed himself to us in the Incarnation of Jesus Christ. So the first part of the book will try to relate this idea of worship, stemming from and centring upon God, to the situation of a congregation which includes all age-groups. The reader will not find a developed theology of worship nor a thorough-going investigation into liturgy, but rather a non-specialist approach to the dynamics of worship in the real situation of twentieth-century church life.

Part One, then, forms the basis for the rest of the book, which is clearly intended as a handbook for leaders of family worship, cleric or lay. Those who are not specifically leaders of worship, but have a concern for the worship of the Church (e.g. Church Councillors) should also find something of interest and of help.

The book is therefore very largely practical. Some may feel that the ideas and suggestions put forward are obvious and the tone didactic. Our concern, however, has been to make the points clear and precise, not to lay down the law. The authors are not attempting to prescribe what is good for the Church so much as to provide material which we hope will be taken with large pinches of the salt of common sense. Our suggestions will therefore need adapting, modifying, moulding and above all discussing before they can be of any use.

We offer this book at a time when the Church is setting out in new directions. We hope that it will help to guide Christian people as they explore new ways in worship.

4

INTRODUCTION

The very considerable growth in recent years of the number of churches holding 'Family Services' of one kind or another is evidence that many people are attracted to forms of worship in which young and old, parents and children can join together. Such forms of worship, however, vary enormously in style, quality and effectiveness. The so-called 'Family Service' is not above criticism, nor is it a panacea for all the Church's ills. However, when young and old, parents and children are allowed and encouraged to meet together for worship, they can enter into an experience which can be both moving and enriching for everyone involved in it.

A man who came to church ostensibly to bring his little girl, but also because he was himself seeking faith, said to the minister at the end of the service: 'When you are taking a service, do you think that everyone in the congregation believes as you believe?' The minister was able to answer 'No', because it is quite plain that in any Christian congregation every person's experience and every person's expectations must be different.

It is important, then, that a church service at which people of all ages are present should allow every worshipper to respond, each in his own way, to the mystery of God's presence. That response must not be stifled or distracted by forms of worship which are trite or ill-conceived, for no one can be nourished in the faith on a diet of shallow cheeriness masquerading as Christian joy.

It is the 'mix' of ages and abilities which constitutes the chief problem for those who are ordering family worship. Although in this book we are aware of this, and offer various suggestions for coping with 'all ages' in church, no easy solution is to be found. We would assert, however, that it is precisely in our *differences* one from another that we find the most precious thing we have to contribute in worship, as with one another we offer ourselves (whatever our age or ability) to God. It is important, therefore, not to skate over or ignore in our worship the differences in experience and expectation within the all-age congregation, for the joy of a congregation in which all ages worship together is that there can be a full and free acceptance of one another.

In order that this may happen, and that each worshipper, whatever his or her age or level of commitment and discipleship, may be led in church towards that encounter with the living God which is the essence of worship 'in spirit and in truth', much more attention needs to be paid by those leading family worship to the liturgical ingredients of their services . . . the place of the Bible, the Sacraments, the preaching and teaching. Churches and congregations differ enormously in the value they place on these things. In some congregations the Eucharist will be taken as the natural setting for Family Worship, while others might see non-eucharistic services as offering greater scope. In fact, experience suggests that eucharistic worship is an entirely appropriate setting for all-age or 'family' services. It will be important, though, for every con-gregation to learn how to make the most of its own particular tradition.

As in church we lay hold on the love of God together, a community of very varied individuals, we need to reflect on the real-life experience of those individuals and the contribution which they can make to the worshipping life of the church. The Church is a body of people on pilgrimage. The route we travel is uneven, and frequently we stumble. Provided, however, that we travel as a worshipping community, honestly seeking ways in which we may advance towards a lively spiritual understanding, then we may be taken unawares by the living God, who comes to meet us where we are, and whose presence makes the place where we are standing holy ground.

PART ONE—IN PRINCIPLE

page

Chapter 1. What do we mean by 'Family Worship'?

The use of the word 'family' as an adjective describing church services is very widespread; 'Family Service' — 'Family Communion' — 'Family Worship' — these titles appear on church notice-boards all over the country, and reports indicate that, wherever these services take place, more and more people are being attracted to attend the church. Obviously 'family' services are fulfilling some kind of need. Their advocates would argue that the family service has brought parents and children to church, perhaps because the service is less formal and easier to understand. On the other hand, there are many critics who would say that family services are offering a watered-down version of the liturgy and theology and are lowering the standards.

There is no reconciling these two views, but in this book we would put forward another thesis altogether: namely, that the experience of a church service in which all ages are worshipping together in the fullest possible participation is a new and rewarding experience for the Church which needs to be worked out in positive terms as a definite contribution to the life of the Church as a whole. As such, the family service stands alongside other services or acts of worship in the church, and does not replace them. The total worship programme of a church may well include the family service as a weekly, monthly, or occasional act of worship, but just because this service attracts more people is no justification for discontinuing services of other kinds. The two or three gathered together in the Lord's name can worship just as effectively (though in a different way) as the two or three hundred.

In our attempts to understand the dynamics of family worship, it is necessary to realise that the adjective 'family' is not the only one which may be used in the description of the kind of worship it seeks to define. The other two adjectives which we use in this book are 'all-age' and 'integrated'. As we are still in the exploratory stages of this particular worship experience, we use these three words interchangeably. While we realise that they are not synonymous, each one is suitable in its context and their definition should become clearer as we go along. We are tempted, too, to put them in inverted commas whenever they appear, but this would make the typography too fussy because of the frequency of their appearance. The reader should understand, however, that whenever the words 'family', 'all-age', or 'integrated' are used as adjectives to describe worship, he should imagine them as set in inverted commas. This indicates that they are in part technical terms, and their descriptive value is therefore limited.

The use of the words 'all-age' or 'integrated' is a deliberate attempt to find some alternative to the word 'family', because this adjective can be ambiguous or even quite inaccurate when applied to a church service. For instance, in church, the family could mean either father, mother and children, or it could mean the family of God. So if you are attending, or responsible for, family worship at your church, you need to ask the question: 'Does *all* the family come to church together, in fact?' If the answer is 'no' (as frequently it must be) then is this really a family service?

Alternatively, can the congregation at a family service really claim to be the family of God? What is the family of God? If it is 'the whole family in heaven and on earth' (Ephesians 3.14) which as the writer says derives its name from the One Heavenly Father, then every act of worship is a family service, regardless of the age of the worshippers or the style of the service.

Probably, if the point were pressed, a minister would say that the family service is an attempt to enable the particular congregation who attend it, old or young, to worship together as a family, and leave it at that. But we should want to go further and ask—'What does it mean to worship as a family?' It may be that we need to await the appearance of a developed theology of the family before we can find an answer to that question. Meanwhile, however, it will suffice to draw attention to the danger of using the title 'family services' to make the Church's worship sound like a nice cosy activity to which young children can be brought. We suspect that this is often the case, and the critics would be quite correct in their assumption that such worship can offer little or nothing in the way of Christian challenge or stimulus.

Having said that, the idea or analogy of the family can be of considerable value, provided that we are *honest*. Honesty compels one to admit that the family as a social unit is not by any means the nice, peaceful, caring set-up that a notice advertising a family service might sometimes imply. In her book *What is a family?* (Hodder and Stoughton) Edith Schaeffer compares the family to a mobile: 'In so many ways (she writes) a family is a mobile—an artwork that takes years, even generations, to produce, but which is never finished. The artwork of this mobile called "family" continues, and imagination, creativity, originality, talent, concern, love, compassion, excitement, determination, and time produce a diversity which is a challenge to any intelligent human being who has been given understanding of how to begin in the studio of life itself' (p.18). And at the end of the book (p.254) the author describes 'a family—for better or for worse' with two great lists of curses and blessings ranging from chicken-pox, anger, depression and toothpaste-tops–left–off to hugs, increasing togetherness, welcomed babies and someone–to–bring–news–to.

We should want to ask whether this kind of dynamic understanding of the family as constantly changing and developing rather than as an institution informs the thinking of those who plan family worship.

Or again, if we reflect on the New Testament teaching, starting from Ephesians 3.14 we find ourselves taking the point that the natural family of man exists in a context of division, strife and conflicting interests, whether between races and nations, or between social or ethnic groups, or within the family unit as we know it, or even within the individual personality. Yet alongside this situation we find the Body of Christ, the Family of God, containing a certain kind of people with a certain kind of destiny. In the course of fulfilling that destiny, this Church/Family, while being totally honest about itself as part of the natural family of mankind, must apply itself to the unifying task of leading mankind onward and upward unto God. The Church in any congregation must see itself as a constituent part of the 'whole family in heaven and on earth' under the fatherhood of God.

Once more we should want to ask whether our family service congregation is being made aware in its worship of its destiny and of its potential within the purposes of God for his whole family.

The point is that the idea or analogy of 'the family' directs our thinking towards a group of people, large or small, of widely differing ages, abilities and interests, endowed with the natural human tendency to strife, tension and discontent. This, in all honesty, is the Church. Yet at the same time the family has a particular 'integrated-ness' and common life in which the positive values of give-and-take, loyalty, and devotion all have a part to play. This, too, is the Church. We do not need to elaborate this thesis here, but we do need to point out that if family worship is to be taken seriously, then it should in some positive way reflect the reality of the family both socially and theologically, and not become merely a means of filling the church and an excuse for trying out the latest gimmicks.

There are various reasons why a church undertakes to include family services within its worship programme. It may be that a shortage of Sunday school teachers has meant that the children are not otherwise catered for; it may be that there is a desire to integrate the children more closely into the worshipping life of the church. It may be that some parents would rather bring their children to church than send them to Sunday school. It may be that the news is getting round that the family services 'work well' in the neighbouring church and the congregation is looking for a fresh approach.

Whatever the reason, once you start, it soon becomes apparent that there are problems to be solved. The music needs adjustment; toddlers need toilets; adults are, at best distracted, at worst grossly offended by the seeming irreverence of the children. The sermon is too difficult for the children, or too simple for the adults; the carefully prepared visual-aid disintegrates; the calculated joke produces no laughter; the reader fails to turn up; the well-meaning teenager answers all the questions; the churchwarden is ostentatiously looking at his watch.

We shall attempt to grapple with these and other problems in the following sections of the book, but here let us deal in general terms with the basic one, which is that, at the family service, you have all ages at worship together. There is, in fact, no solution to this, so long as it is seen as a problem.

The only way to deal with this is to treat the whole subject, not as a problem, but as a growth-point. Why do we want all ages to worship together? Not just to fill the church, but to allow the differing responses of each age-group to contribute to the total act of worship. If you approach it in this way, then each worshipper has something valuable to offer; the cry or crow of the baby is as valid as the well-modulated tones of the tenor, the unexpected movements of the wandering toddler as meaningful as the procession from the vestry, and the reluctant Amen of the teenager as acceptable as the fervent prayer of the Bible-class leader.

In order that the family service should become an integrated act of worship in spite of the variety of ages present, it requires a particular kind of giving on the part of the church as a whole. The vicar or minister ultimately responsible for the quality of the worship must be flexible—he aims for excellence and yet allows for amateurishness; the church council must be adventurous in allowing experiments; the traditional worshippers must be tolerant of new approaches; the enthusiastic leaders must be ready to temper some of their flights of fancy; the young people and children must be encouraged to learn the lessons of loyalty and good manners. Once you begin to see all-age worship in this light, then it should become clear that a church which is prepared to work at it will find that it is exploring a particular kind of worship experience in which the keynotes will be giving and participation.

Enough has been said to indicate that all-age worship is quite different from 'Children's Church' or 'Junior Church'. We should hope that the family service would replace these as a far more adequate offering of worship. Children and young people are emphatically not to be regarded merely as the Church of the future; they are part of the Church of today, and this truth should be affirmed by incorporating them into an integrated act of worship. It is vitally important, therefore, that the family service should not descend to the 'lowest common denominator' in the quality of its constituent parts just for the sake of the children. Those who plan and lead it have a clear duty to present the Christian truth at all levels. This is certainly a very difficult exercise, and some might say impossible in the context of a family service or even a series of family services. Nevertheless this is the ideal which must be held up in front of those responsible for leadership in all-age worship, or we shall be in danger of presenting the Christian faith in a version so watered-down as to be valueless.

While we must constantly think in terms of the 'ideal' of all-age worship as a positive contribution to the life and development of the Church, we must at the same time be realistic, and recognise that a variety of difficulties present themselves according to the situation of each church which tries it out. We try in the course of this book to deal with some of the 'internal' difficulties such as you might encounter in any particular church set-up, by presenting ideas and methods of approach suitable for integrated worship, which may not have been attempted so far by some congregations. However, it is necessary to take a clear look at the environment in which the church is situated to see whether the all-age worship approach is necessarily the best. Just because it 'works' in parish A, does not mean that it will be successful in parish B.

There could be a population-mix which is unbalanced, perhaps bringing an unusually high proportion of children to the church; or alterna-

B

tively insufficient children to warrant a different approach for their benefit. There may be a preponderance of graduates in the congregation, or possibly a fairly high proportion of inmates from a local home for the mentally-handicapped. Obviously such factors have to be taken into account when considering whether to introduce family worship or when assessing its usefulness after a period of time. There is also the question of potential in terms of leadership; if the church has just not got the sort of leaders who can relate easily and readily to people of all ages, then the family service approach we have under consideration here should probably not be attempted.

Whether or not your church has a family service or is thinking about starting one, it is an excellent idea for a group from the congregation to examine the church's worship. We know that the vicar or minister is ultimately responsible for it, but he would be wise to share this responsibility with a group of worshippers and raise such questions as : what is worship for? how should it be done? who is it for? how could it become more satisfactory or satisfying? what are its essentials? why do we do what we do in church? are there any people who could be asked or trained to assist? if so, what could they do? It could well be that, as a result of such an enquiry, new ideas and leaders could emerge, bringing a fresh experience in worship in the church whether or not it is called a family service.

Chapter 2. Liturgy and its Setting

Although the new styles of worship recommended in this book may often be managed more easily in a modern than in an ancient building, it is nevertheless quite possible for all-age worship to be presented and offered effectively in practically any setting.

If you have an ancient or traditional building, it is a good idea to begin by asking some fundamental questions, such as:

'Why did our forefathers build it like this?'
'What were they trying to say?' (about God, about Jesus, about man, about worship).
'Is there anything we can learn from them?'
'In what ways do we differ from them in our ideas?'

It is important that we should approach the architecture of the past with humility and gratitude, and often with awe and wonder. Yet every generation has new insights and new ways of expressing the faith both in art and in liturgy. So it would be interesting to see how your church building has been constructed, and how it has been altered, by whom, and why. It has been estimated that most parish churches have some major alteration about every 40 years. Does that apply in your case?

Church furnishings as well as church architecture reflect basic assumptions. Can you decide what assumptions are implied about faith and worship by, for example, an altar set right against the east wall, a massive and dominant central pulpit, a font in a corner at the back, fixed pews facing one way, a sanctuary rail, an organ, even a carpet or lack of one? (The fact that no ancient church is provided with a lavatory caused one Church Council considerable concern and amusement when that particular assumption was called in question!)

Such things may have been taken for granted for years, but they come into prominence when we engage in all-age worship which requires a new kind of response from a more fully-participating congregation.

The church building and its furnishings should be discussed at some point by any group which is responsible for planning family services.

15

How it has been altered, by whom and why . . .

In fact, 'Our Church Building' could well become a theme in itself for one or more family services, so that even if the building cannot be altered structurally, at least it can be used for the benefit of the worshippers in a new and imaginative way.

Our concern is to explore new ways in worship to allow for the changing social styles and patterns in church-going. However, any innovations must be closely linked with the traditional forms of worship by which Christians have expressed their relationship to God all down the ages. It is sometimes assumed that family worship must necessarily depart from all traditional patterns of church services, and become a kind of liturgical free-for-all. This is far from the truth.

From the practical point of view, it is better for anyone beginning to experiment with ideas for all-age worship to start by re-working the traditional forms and patterns rather than by trying to write his own service. The reason for this is that there exist certain liturgical principles in Christian worship, and if we depart radically from these, then we shall have little to offer in the way of worship, either to the worshipper or to God. In very simple terms, the principles governing Christian worship could be summarised in this way:

All true worship is God-centred, and God-inspired; but a governing principle of Christian worship is to 'discern the Body of Christ'. This applies whether a service is eucharistic or not (see St Paul's discussion in I Cor. 11.23–29). We take it that the Body of Christ is focused in the eucharistic symbols of bread and wine, but is also to be understood in a social and community sense where the two or three are gathered together in his name. Christian worshippers are necessarily joined together in a loving relationship with one another and the Lord. It is a question of drawing people's attention to who they are when they meet.

There are certain things which, as a matter of principle, Christian people do when they meet together for worship.

They proclaim. It is the joyful task of Christians to proclaim and constantly to re-affirm in their worship the story of what God has done in and through Jesus Christ.

They pray. Worship is an opportunity for 'shared praying', not as a group of private individuals, but as a 'common' or community act.

They read the Bible. Good liturgy gives prime place to the 'making known' of the Bible as God's word to men.

They make an offering. Liturgy includes the response of offering, whereby the worshipper is given the freedom to offer himself to God. Any offertory or collection is symbolic of this free and loving response of the individual who has heard and received God's word in the Gospel.

They react to the setting in which worship takes place. Words are pressed into service in worship, but the liturgy extends beyond what mere words can utter. For this, Christians explore the worlds of the arts, music, architecture and so forth, as further means whereby the inexpressible wonder of God may be expressed.

These things lie beneath the liturgical forms which have come to us from the past, and they need to be taken into account in any experiment we make in the future. If they are ignored or not fully understood and appreciated, then our worship becomes gimmicky and individualistic, an offering which satisfies nobody in the long run.

Now let us take a look at some of the ingredients of the Christian liturgy which can be helpful in the ordering of all-age worship.

Music and poetry

Liturgy seeks to express in earthly terms the inexpressible wonder of God. The use of music and poetry in church is, in a sense, an extension of the uninhibited expression of joy and praise of the Pentecostal speaking-in-tongues. The beauty of music is a tremendous enhancement of worship, but for integrated worship a great deal of attention needs to be paid to the more spontaneous forms of folk music. Here, too, more use could be made of poetry. The Psalms, read instead of chanted, are an obvious example; but there is other religious and secular poetry which, if well read, can add a good deal to the worship experience.

Movement in worship

It is very important, when thinking in terms of all-age worship, to realise that good liturgy is a drama, a kind of re-enactment in dramatic terms of what God has done for mankind. This is seen most obviously in the Eucharist, but should be implicit in every church service, giving it a recognisable shape and purpose.

In this respect, movement plays a very important part. Many churches today are experimenting with liturgical dance as one way of high-lighting the importance of movement in contributing towards the total drama of the liturgy, but other kinds of movement need to be recognised as being of some significance. For instance, the movement of people going to church, finding a seat (or being shown to one), standing up and kneeling, bringing banners or flags to church, going forward to receive Holy Communion, even moving to another part of the church or hall for coffee, all these are significant actions.

Once this is recognised, then it becomes possible to think in terms of other significant movements within the context of the service itself, especially by younger people (some of whom cannot sit still for long periods), e.g. action songs, prepared or 'instant' drama or dance, the Pax, processions, stations of the cross or similar 'excursions'. At the same time, the movements of the leaders, celebrant, choir, servers, etc. will merit a closer study as to their significance. The actions of the President of the Eucharist, of course, deserve careful attention to see that they are meaningful and a real part of the whole act of worship—

not just something he does for his own private reasons or because he doesn't know what to do with his hands!

Light and colour
Light and colour within the architectural setting of liturgy is something we normally take for granted. A church must have windows and lights. Yet we need to be more conscious of light and colour in all-age worship, partly because both contribute to the 'atmosphere', and partly because young people in particular are very sensitive to them. Stained glass windows make their point in a rather uncompromising way (though their significance has been considerably stretched in many post-war churches which have good modern glass, specifically, of course, in Coventry Cathedral); but we can be more liturgically alive to the possibilities of colour e.g. in the use of vestments, banners, pulpit-falls, curtain fabrics, flowers, even on the notice-board; and of light by the use of candles and candle-lighting and special services in which light plays an important part, e.g. The Easter Vigil, Advent, Candlemas, The Transfiguration.

Symbols
Whereas most of the intellectual concepts which crowd into our worship through the written and spoken word can only appeal to the older and better-educated members of our congregations, symbols have a ready appeal to worshippers of all ages and abilities. The symbolic nature of the Christian liturgy is to be seen at almost every point in a well-ordered act of worship. The walk to the church, significant of the desire to meet the Lord in company with other Christians; the music, symbolic of the joy in believing; the words of the Bible read and expounded, symbolic of the self-revelation of the hidden God; the words of prayers and the attitudes of the worshippers, symbolic of the hopes and needs of the people both inside and outside the church; the collection, symbolic of our desire to give back to God something of his own creation; the sacraments with their own powerful symbolism of the great saving acts of God in Christ.

All these point to the inescapable fact that true Christian worship is an activity of the heart (feelings and emotions) at least as much as an activity of the brain (thinking/intellect). In this respect, then, children and young people have as much to offer as adults—possibly more, because the 'feeling' side of their nature dominates the intellectual side, and they may well understand the things of God intuitively in a way that many adults cannot.

All-age worship, then, must be alive to the great importance and possibilities of the symbols of the liturgy. It is not necessary (or desirable) to explain everything. Worship was never intended to be instantly understandable. Nor, indeed, need it be deliberately obscure. The traditional Christian symbols can bear a certain amount of commentary, but they must also on occasions be allowed to speak for themselves.

Unusual symbolic actions can sometimes be used to great effect for particular occasions, e.g. an outside Palm Sunday procession of witness with a live donkey . . . lighting of a bonfire outside the church door (if it is safe!) on Easter Eve, distribution of christingles at Advent or of flowers on Mothering Sunday. Such actions, however, need to relate closely and positively to biblical and Christian teaching. If careful thought is not taken, they could lead to unfortunate results; as in the church where the vicar introduced the symbolic washing of *hands* (instead of feet) for Maundy Thursday, apparently oblivious of the fact that he was involving his congregation in the symbolic gesture used by Pilate to try and rid himself of the guilt of Jesus's death.

Preaching

The use of the sermon in worship has caused much criticism during the last 25 years. It is, nevertheless, an integral part of the liturgy. The highest aim is to captivate a congregation of all ages by one's enthusiasm for the Gospel. Preaching may include story-telling, demonstrations, and visual aids. Yet it must still be preaching, and the preacher must still be as eloquent as he can in proclaiming and expounding the word of God. The preacher is his own best audio-visual aid, and there is no better way of communicating the Gospel than by the witness of his own personal testimony to the faith.

Common Prayer

It is important that those who introduce more flexible forms of worship should remember the importance of common prayer as one of the liturgical foundations. Common prayer does not mean prayers said by the people together, although these may indeed happen. It is, rather, prayers which seek to make expression of the 'common' or 'community' personality of the worshippers. Such prayers, if they are well constructed (as, for example, the Collects) gain by repetition and learning by heart, whether they are said by one person on behalf of all who are gathered together, or whether they are recited in chorus by the whole congregation or a section of it.

It doesn't matter a great deal if such prayers are not in modern English. The majority of ancient prayers are not nearly so difficult to understand as modern reformers often allege, and the meaning can grow and deepen for worshippers who become familiar with them.

And finally . . .
It may be thought that in the ensuing sections of the book, some of the more novel ideas which are put forward as suggestions verge on gimmickry. Whether or not any particular idea becomes a gimmick will depend very largely on how it is presented. Certainly, gimmickry in church is to be deplored for the very good reason that worship is not, and must never become, an entertainment. In using illustrative material of any kind, the aid must be first and foremost to illuminate the theme. We suggest that this may be done quite boldly and imaginatively in various ways which may not have been tried before in church.

Some kind of evaluation is always needed. If in the end you hear remarks like: 'I found it very helpful to think about the Holy Spirit in that way'—then the illustration (whatever it might have been) was probably valid and useful. If all you hear is: 'I did enjoy that bit when you let off those balloons!'—then your illustration, however well-intended, would have to be classed as gimmickry.

Chapter 3. Leadership: Some General Observations

Whatever we may hear about 'unstructured' worship, there can really be no such thing. Human beings naturally group themselves into structures of one kind or another. All-age worship is not an 'un-structuring' of traditional worship patterns; it is a 're-structuring' of them. Consequently the question of leadership is of great significance.

The traditional patterns of English worship tend to mirror the hierarchical structures of society in the past. This may not be a bad thing, in that it can produce a well-ordered and dignified act of worship, centring on the priest, minister or celebrant, in which everyone knows his or her place in church. It must be recognised, however, that the role of most of the participants in such worship tends to be a subordinate one. Pictorially, this situation might be represented in the form of a pyramid:

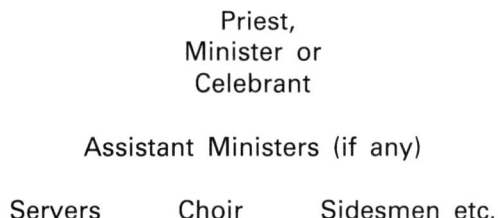

Priest,
Minister or
Celebrant

Assistant Ministers (if any)

Servers   Choir   Sidesmen etc.

The 'ordinary' men, women and children in the pew

Many so-called family services do little or nothing to alter this structure; but if a family service is really to become all-age, integrated, common (community) worship, then its leadership needs to be reconsidered. The aim is to lead people away from passive subordination and towards active participation in the worship of God. This will more truly mirror the situation in contemporary society and should provide a more familiar point of reference and therefore relevance for twentieth-century worshippers. To achieve this, it will be necessary to take a wider view of who is involved in the processes of planning and organisation of the family service. The re-structuring for the actual church service itself is best expressed in terms of the diagram on p. 23.

```
                    LEADER
        VICAR or    / | \
        MINISTER   /  |  \        HELPERS FOR
       /           \  |   \       PRAYERS        SUNDAY
SERVER(S)           \ |    \      READINGS       SCHOOL
                     \|     X     VISUAL AIDS etc.
         CONGREGATION      / \
        /                 /   \
SIDESMEN                 MUSICIAN(S)
STEWARDS etc.
```

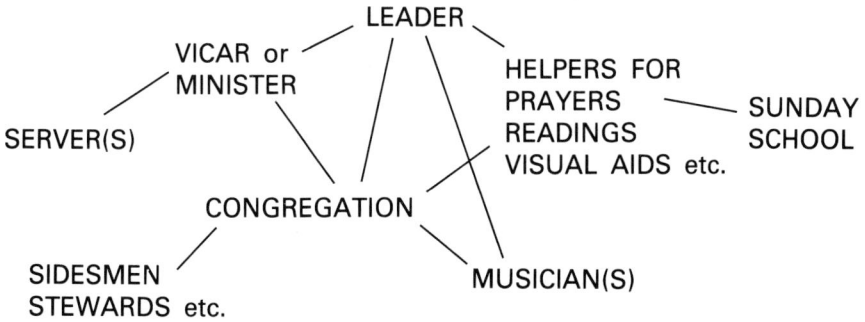

In all-age worship, someone has to be firmly in control; we prefer to call that person the leader. He (or she) may or may not be the minister of the church or parish, according to circumstances; but the point should be stressed that the leader *need not* be an ordained person. The first qualification for the leader of all-age worship is his or her ability to relate fairly readily to people of all ages. This is a skill which can be acquired, and clergy should be quick to notice anyone in the congregation who could be trained to lead worship in this way. Such people need to be invited to take part in any planning and assessing, and also encouraged to take part in church services generally, so that they get the 'feel' of the thing in terms of voice production, control of movement, congregational response and so on.

The second diagram indicates that the vicar or minister is not necessarily the leader for any particular service. Although he is obviously responsible for what goes on in the church, the amount of overt leadership he actually exercises in the service will vary greatly according to the local situation. A good deal of thought needs to be given to the assessment of key people in the church and their ability and willingness to stand up in front of others.

A ready response from the congregation during the course of the service is more likely to occur if the vicar or minister is available while people are coming in to church. Whenever possible, he should be ready with a friendly greeting and a word for the children, without overdoing it. Possibly he may be able to direct people's attention to displays of visual material relating to the theme of the service. A little tact and imagination is needed to make the best of this precious 15 minutes before the service actually begins but, by that time, the vicar should have demonstrated that he is on speaking terms with at least some of the congregation.

In his capacity as administrative head of the church, the vicar or minister will no doubt need to talk about church business with other officials. This should properly be done *after* the service, not before.

One of the problems of writing a book of this kind, which contains ideas and suggestions for worship, is that it is rather easy to give a false impression of unqualified success. The ideas, suggestions and practical advice which we put forward are bound to be descriptive of what has been successful and has 'worked' in various church situations, but it would not be difficult to produce a book of equal proportions cataloguing the frustrations and disappointments which most of those engaged in leading worship have experienced at one time or another. So the following remarks are included as a corrective at this stage, for the authors would be the first to admit that the road which leads to truly integrated worship is strewn with frustrations, arguments and failures.

It is right, therefore, to refer to the *cost* of leadership as a shared experience of both clergy and lay people who are trying to make the liturgy 'come alive' for a congregation of mixed ages and abilities.

For some clergy, the cost may make itself felt in terms of a new insecurity. Merely to be out of the pulpit, or away from a remote sanctuary and amongst the people instead, can produce a feeling of vulnerability which may be quite difficult for a priest or minister to come to terms with. Another 'area of pain' could well be having to endure on occasions a second-rate presentation of part of the service by a semi-trained lay person, when the clergyman knows he could do it so much better himself. Alternatively, of course, there may come the pride-swallowing moment when superlative praise follows an address by a lay person, praise which the clergyman may not have received for some years.

The letting-go of cherished functions may be a costly business for some clergy, for when lay people begin to participate more fully in the liturgy, they begin to ask questions which might be difficult to answer with any logical authority: e.g. 'Does a priest really *have* to be the only person to handle the Sacraments, or the altar vessels?'; 'Does the pulpit *have* to be occupied by an ordained or duly authorised person?'; 'Does

24

the minister *have* to preach for more than ten minutes?' In integrated worship, the clergyman may feel he is surrendering control, and this requires both courage and humility.

It is suggested that all-age worship should be arranged as far as possible with a built-in opportunity for open criticism. The encouraging of critical attitudes and the handling of criticism are both costly operations. In some instances, the introduction of all-age worship will cause tension and raise all kinds of anxieties. Some people with status positions within the church (organist, choirmaster, MC, churchwarden, steward, trustee, Sunday school superintendent, to mention a few) may feel threatened, and may express quite forcibly their feelings of anxiety and resentment at the changes that are taking place. Some people may even leave the church.

All this is costly to a sensitive pastor, who must be able not only to cope personally with such problems, but also to recognise the cost to others of introducing new patterns of worship. He must be able to use his discernment to sift out genuine distress from mere superficial bitterness.

The awesome shock of standing up in front of a congregation for the first time . . .

25

Lay people who begin to take part in the leading of worship will also have to be prepared to understand something of the costs of leadership. In their case, it may be the awesome shock of standing up in front of a congregation for the first time. Once that is overcome, lay leaders need to count the cost in terms of time taken to prepare for worship, and then in sharing the burdens of criticism and failure.

They may also find that because of the effort they have put into any particular service, they themselves seem to be deprived of the very spiritual refreshment they hope to enable others to receive. This can be a real problem and the planning group should discuss this question and see whether it would be sensible to arrange some alternative devotional exercise for leaders—a week-day Communion, perhaps, or a short time away together at a retreat house or similar centre.

All this may sound a little depressing, but we have deliberately shown the darker side of the picture so that clergy and leaders who do run into difficulties in the re-ordering of worship may realise that they are not alone in this, and it is no reason for giving up. In general, however, it is true to say that church groups who engage in planning family worship find that the difficulties are far outweighed by the new experience of joy in worship, and by the bonds of Christian fellowship which are forged and strengthened in the process of working together for the real benefit of the congregation and community.

Chapter 4. Teamwork: People as a Resource

To begin with, we need to refer back to the second diagram in the previous chapter on page 23. It is intended as a kind of model for church organisation as it applies to the ordering of integrated family worship. If you are looking for resources in order to introduce family worship in your church, then you begin by looking at people. For it will be essential to assemble some kind of team of people of varying talents before any further progress can be made.

The implications of the word 'team' cannot be over-emphasised. Obviously, the vicar or minister is a key person, but however enthusiastic and imaginative an approach a parish priest has to his family services, he cannot be expected to produce original ideas fifty-two weeks in the year. Some clergy are aware that they are not at their best in this situation and wisely hand over this part of their work to those lay people with the necessary talents, taking care to ensure that their own interest and support are obvious and sincere.

In sharing the various tasks which need to be done in and around a family service, care needs to be taken to see that these are not so simple, dull and monotonous as to afford little opportunity for spiritual development, or that it is only the 'bright' ones who get the important jobs. Even the youngest children must be given the opportunity to participate at some point, though not necessarily in every service.

We know that visual aids are of great value in focusing attention or summarising a theme. It is here that the teenage and adult members of the congregation can profitably be called upon to help. Use your carpenters, your needleworkers, your artists, your electricians, hi-fi boffins, photographers, printers, lighting experts and musicians in order to produce the banners, posters, props, and sound and lighting effects that will help transform an ordinary service into a memorable act of worship.

It will often be found that the planning and preparation stages of a particular service, if done carefully, can be as meaningful and valuable as the presentation itself. The leader can then use preparatory meetings as adult training sessions, particularly if some of the people involved are inexperienced. Sometimes this training can be aimed at enriching the group's spiritual development through bible-study and discussion; at other times it may have a practical bias and include the construction of visual aids or advice in handling audio-visual equipment.

It must be remembered, however, that not everyone may want to become involved in this way, and care must be taken not to embarrass people by insisting that they take a more active role, or by making them feel inadequate if they do not. Some recognition must be given to the fact that their very presence in church is a valuable 'resource bank'. At a family service you are likely to find the combined presence of pre-school toddlers, primary-age children, adolescents, young marrieds, the middle-aged and the elderly. Their prayerfulness and the attention they give to what is happening are generating an atmosphere which can be a valuable contribution to real worship.

Granny brings with her to church four generations of loving care which, together with the experience of the middle-aged, the optimism of the young marrieds, the diffidence or energy of the teenagers, the curiosity of the juniors and the freshness of the four-year-olds, combine to demonstrate the continuous renewal of God's creation.

PART TWO—IN CHURCH

Section 1. Drafting an Order of Service

When drafting an order of service for all-age family worship it is best to bear in mind the principal features of Christian liturgical worship outlined in Part 1 Chapter 2 (see page 17). These features are summed up as Proclamation, Prayer, Scripture and Offering, all taking place in a liturgical setting (i.e. the church building and congregation) to which worshippers react.

Family services have often been justly accused of being an inadequate offering of worship, merely a hymn-prayer-reading sandwich with a talk thrown in. If this accusation is deserved, it is probably because those responsible for ordering the service have not taken sufficient trouble to match their order of service against the underlying principles which guide Christian worship in general.

To sum up very briefly what this implies:
> The Proclamation of the Good News should be clear and joyful;
> The Prayer should speak for the people;
> The Scriptures should be honoured;
> The Offering should imply self-oblation;

and, in addition, the people should be given the opportunity to react to the setting, 'catching' something of the atmosphere and relating to their fellow-worshippers. Any satisfactory order of service will therefore allow for all this to happen as a matter of course.

A well-ordered service will always contain climaxes. These need to be thought about and built into the order of service if they are not already provided, as they are in a baptism, or in a Eucharist. In most services, the sermon is a natural climax. If it is the only one, then it should not take place too early, because the climax should be in the latter part of the service. Most family services will not need more than two high points of this kind.

The only other basic factor which needs to be borne in mind in drafting an order of service is to see that it provides a reasonable variety: a good mixture of music and spoken word, of standing and sitting (and kneeling), of opportunities for joining in and also for remaining still. A commonsense middle course has to be found between too frequent changes on the one hand, and too much of one thing on the other. Only careful monitoring and honest criticism will indicate when the design is about right.

We are setting out here only two basic orders for a family service. They are frameworks, Form A non-eucharistic and Form B eucharistic, which need to be looked at alongside other orders to fill them out or adapt them according to local circumstance and custom. Leaders who are looking for other forms of service should be able to find what they need if they follow up the suggested resource material in Part 3 Section 9.

Form A (non-eucharistic)

1. Introduction
   — includes Procession of choir, ministers, colours etc; welcome; statement of theme; call to worship; opening sentence(s)

2. The first hymn
   — this should be a well-known one; if it is customary for the collection to be taken during a hymn, it should be during this one, but not offered yet (see No. 5); otherwise it should be taken just before or just after this hymn

3. Reading and Listening
   — the lessons are read here, with whatever interlude (e.g. hymn, canticle, anthem, silence) is felt to be appropriate between them and after them

4. The Church's Prayers
   — the more formal prayers, which could include the Creed, The Lord's Prayer, Responses, Collects

5. The Offering
   — the gifts (collection and any other gifts) of the people are brought to the front and presented for blessing with appropriate prayer or sentence

6. The second (or third) hymn

7. The Sermon and Informal Prayers
   — the order of these could be reversed. Some informal singing could be introduced in this section. (The Sermon could alternatively be placed immediately after Section 3)

8. The Notices

9. The final hymn

10. The conclusion
    — could include a prayer of dedication, the Blessing, a form of dismissal, procession out.

Form B (eucharistic)

1. Introduction
   — will include Procession of choir, ministers, colours; welcome; statement of theme; opening prayer e.g. Collect for purity

2. The first hymn
   — this should be a well-known one; if it is customary for the collection to be taken during a hymn, it should be during this one, but not offered yet (see No. 8); otherwise it should be taken just before or just after this hymn

3. The Collect of the Day

4. Reading and Listening
   — the lessons, epistle, gospel, are read here, with whatever interlude (e.g. hymn, canticle, anthem, silence) is felt to be appropriate between them and after them.

5. The Sermon

6. The second hymn

7. The Prayers
   — these may be formal or informal and include any preparation for communion which is felt to be necessary

8. The Offertory
   — this may be preceded by The Peace; the offerings of bread, wine and money (and any other gifts) are brought to the front and offered with appropriate sentence or prayer

9. The third hymn
   — during this the altar is prepared for communion

10. The Communion
    — includes the eucharistic prayer, the Lord's Prayer and other prayers according to custom, and the general communion; the post-communion prayer

11. The Notices

12. The Final hymn

13. The Conclusion
   — the Blessing, dismissal, procession out according to custom.

A Note on Baptism

Any existing order for a Baptism service can be expanded into a family service simply by inserting hymns, prayers and a sermon in appropriate places and including a dignified procession to and from the font.

If it were desired to combine a Baptism with Form A, it would be best to insert the Promises and Baptism proper in place of item 4, and ensure that item 7 is not too long. The Reception could follow the Baptism immediately or be included in item 7 to give it some emphasis.

If Baptism is to be combined with the Eucharist, it is best to dispense with the sermon as such altogether, and insert the Promises and Baptism and Reception together at item 5 in Form B. Again, item 7 should be kept short or even omitted altogether.

These remarks apply equally to Infant and Adult Baptism services. A similar re-ordering of the service could take place to accommodate other infant ceremonies within the liturgy, such as Child Thanksgiving and the Blessing or Dedication of a child.

Section 2. Practical Hints for Leaders

What is his job?

The leader of the family service will be responsible for introducing the service, making the announcements and any commentary that is needed, inviting the congregation to sing, make responses, and sit, stand or kneel as appropriate. If the service is the Eucharist, the leader may be the celebrant. If he is not celebrating, he could well be responsible for the whole of the ministry of the word. At all events, he will seek to enhance the atmosphere of Christian friendliness and fellowship, making people feel at ease as much as possible.

How does he do it?

By breaking the ice . . . it is very easy for a kind of frosty inhibition to settle over any formal gathering, and church services are all too prone to this. All-age worship will not achieve its best results unless the ice of British Christian reserve is at least partially thawed. It is the leader's job to thaw it. Having said that, it is very difficult to specify how it should be done, because every church and congregation has its own particular characteristics, and therefore each requires a different approach. In general, however, the more successful leader will be the person who is genuine and sincere in his faith, has a good grasp of the principles of worship, and who is friendly and good-humoured.

Some personal rapport should be established between the leader and members of the congregation before the service actually starts, perhaps simply by an informal chat with one or two people as they come into church. From there, the leader has to introduce the theme of the service at an appropriate moment as near to the beginning of the service as possible.

He should do this as informally as possible, e.g. 'Good morning! Today is the second Sunday after the Epiphany. Some churches call it Plough Sunday and in the country they might say special prayers for the farmers ploughing the fields. Some of us have been looking at those pictures on display at the back of the church. They show how Christian Aid is trying to help people who haven't enough to eat. Later on in our service, we shall be thinking a bit more about hungry people' (NOT 'about poverty and hunger'—it is better to use concrete rather than abstract expressions) 'and Derek and Jane are going to sing a song about this. But now we are ready to start the service; so here is Brian to light the candles and the choir and servers and priest are coming in to take their places.'

Thinking about hungry people . . .

This would class as a very lightweight 'ice-breaker'—but it may be necessary to work a little harder, yet without lengthening the introduction too much. For instance, a visitor could be introduced (perhaps a new family, or a visiting speaker, or even a new baby) or a very brief question-and-answer session could be used.

It is worth repeating that the leader should be ready with a *smile*, and *look* at the congregation when he is speaking to them. This is something to do with the freedom of the leader. A good leader has an in-built sense of freedom which allows him to enjoy being with and relating to the congregation. This freedom means that he will be able to communicate something of his enjoyment to the people.

By being in the right place . . . in all-age worship, the symbols of altar, pulpit and lectern need to be recognised as somehow belonging to the

36

whole congregation, not confined to the priest or minister. Thus, in the eucharistic family service, the altar will (if possible) be fairly close to the people (if not actually amongst them) and children will accompany the communicants and receive a blessing if not the sacrament itself. And in non-eucharistic worship, the ministry of the Word of God will not be a prescription from on high so much as a shared experience.

Remembering this, the leader will not always be able to 'hide behind' the lectern or pulpit or prayer-desk. He will have to move about a bit. This may be necessary simply in order to 'include everyone in'—for instance the choir or those in side aisles; or possibly as a strategy at some point in the service such as taking a group of children to show them something, going to the centre or to the back to lead prayers, giving out pictures, texts, or other objects, collecting names for intercession. For the most part, however, the leader's 'base camp' will be somewhere where he can be seen and heard easily by all in church, presumably somewhere near the front and not too exalted. The art in all this is to be able to move about purposefully, yet at the same time to avoid restlessness which can be very distracting.

By taking care with the announcements . . . the key-word here is 'friendly'. In the relatively formal atmosphere of most churches (especially if the congregation is fairly large) it is very easy to become stereotyped and rather grim. 'We will now sing hymn numbah two-hundred and three; the two-hundred and third hymn!' Variations of this technique abound (much to the delight of comedians!)—but such announcements can drown all-age worship in a deluge of formality before it has a chance to come to life.

Why not be friendly, *smile*, and say: 'Now it's time to sing our first (next) hymn. It's number 203, and when you've found the place, we'll just have a look at the words of the first two lines; two-oh-three.' It is usually necessary to repeat the number clearly; the slightest cough can obscure it the first time, and there may be people with hearing defects, or youngsters with wandering thoughts.

A good leader uses his eyes a lot. There is no need to stare; but every member of the congregation should know that the leader has seen him. A leader who is aware in this way will soon know whether his announcement has been heard and understood.

Great care has to be taken when combining two or more announcements: if you say 'We are going to take the collection during the next hymn. The hymn will be number 197', by the time you get to the number, a large part of the congregation will be searching for money and will miss the number. Better to say, 'Have your collection ready because Jim and Susan are going to take it during the next hymn.' Then announce the number when most people are ready.

Likewise with other directives. 'Now we are going to stand and say together the Apostles' Creed which you will find on page 8.' This has got to be: 'We're going to say the Apostles' Creed. It's on page 8' (Pause while they find it). 'Would you please stand up'. If you mention the word 'stand' and then go on talking, some will begin to stand before you've completed the announcement.

By inviting criticism . . . there is no need to state the obvious about being heard and seen and not fiddling with your right ear while talking. The best thing is for every leader to have a critic in the congregation. There may be people who would not want to be part of a planning team but who could make a valuable contribution to the worship by being constructive critics. A planning and assessing group could assist in this, but perhaps just as effective is the child who says . . . 'Daddy, why DO you stand on one one leg when you're talking?' . . . or the wife who remarks 'I kept wondering if you were going to trip over your cassock!'

By rounding off the service . . . the leader could do this by simply stating 'After the blessing, the service is over, and we all go home, or over into the hall for a cup of coffee'—or he could use a less formal method, and when the choir have gone to the back, he could take a couple of willing young volunteers to extinguish the candles, or a group to have another look at the visual display material. Before doing this, he may say something like: 'Mrs Smith and her helpers are ready with refreshments, so if you're not in a hurry to go home, come along for a few moments of Christian fellowship.'

These are practical considerations with regard to details of leadership in worship. It needs to be realised, though, that a leader communicates something of his own 'life in God' to the congregation in some indefinable way as he or she stands before a congregation even before any word is uttered. Every leader of worship, therefore, has to work continually at his own spiritual preparation for the task; without this, all technical expertise is valueless.

Section 3. Practical Hints for the Rest of the Team

Readers

It is common practice today for lay people to be responsible for reading the lessons, and this we would recommend for family worship. Having said that, it is important to realise that not everyone has the ability to read well in church. Lessons must be read audibly and in such a way as to make people listen and reflect. Bad reading is an embarrassment.

Bearing this in mind, the following points may be helpful when rehearsing readers:

1. *Wait* for a few moments for attention before beginning to read.

2. Read *slowly* with consonants well-enunciated.

3. *Look* at the congregation from time to time. In ordinary conversation, those who look at you while they are speaking command your attention; this also applies when speaking or reading to a congregation.

4. Read with *'colour'*; i.e. aim for reasonable variations in tone, pitch, pace and volume.

5. Be *visible*; i.e. don't hide behind the book or lectern. (Smaller people should be provided with a firm stool or platform.)

6. Be *sensitive* to the acoustics, making allowance for resonance or 'deadness' in the building. (If amplification is used, it must be good equipment.)

7. Beware of voice mannerisms; e.g. the 'parsonical' sing-song voice.

Obviously it will be helpful to have a friendly critic, both for rehearsals and 'on the day'. It may be possible to enlist the help of someone trained in elocution to give advice.

Have you ever thought . . . of having a group to do the reading? Some readings (e.g. the Passion) can be presented very effectively by more than one reader, either standing together at the front, or from different parts of the church (but warn the congregation in advance or they will be too busy looking for the readers to listen to the reading!). It is also possible to sort out a number of short passages from the Bible to illustrate a particular theme and give them to different people to read, e.g. if your service theme is 'Light', look up the word 'Light' in a concordance, and select appropriate verses from the Old and New Testaments.

... of using different translations of the Bible from the one you normally use? Sometimes it is a good idea to announce which translation is being used. (Note: amidst the plethora of modern alternatives, the King James version should not be forgotten altogether. It still speaks in its own special way to the twentieth-century congregation.)

... of using non-biblical readings? They need to be chosen for their excellence and relevance to the theme of the service.

... of providing plastic covers for the sheets of paper if readings have to be typed or written out? It is often easier, if you are using a non-biblical reading, or an 'edited' biblical reading, to type out the reading in advance. Simple A4-size transparent plastic folders can be purchased for a few pence from any good stationer; they provide an excellent cover for a typed reading, and prevent the paper from rustling.

Musicians
The organist could be asked to say a word about a particular hymn or piece of music. The choir, or a soloist, could be asked to sing while we listen and think about the words.

Bell-Ringers
They could be invited to be introduced to the congregation. One of them could be asked (interviewed?) about bell-ringing. A family service could be based on the theme of 'Bells'—remembering their function as signalling joy, or warning, or inviting to worship, or marking the passing of time. (The fact that a bell has to be in tune with itself and with the other bells is a kind of parable for Christian living!)

Teachers, Helpers and Volunteers
These are people drawn in to assist in presenting a demonstration. They may be people with a specialist knowledge (e.g. the policeman in the idea on page 115) prepared in advance, or an *ad hoc* 'volunteer' called from the congregation in the middle of the talk. In using the latter, care must be taken not to embarrass people by asking them to participate against their will.

Foster People
These are any of the good-hearted people in the congregation who are prepared to help mothers with their children during the service. It is all very well saying that children are welcome but they can still sometimes become an embarrassment to their mothers, even in the most informal

service. The 'foster people' can often help to solve this problem by sitting with the family, or taking care of one particular child if there are several in the family. Usually the foster people will carry on their work as unobtrusively as possible, but it may be desirable to draw attention to them once in a while. (The foster people may well also be the people who look after the Baptism Roll, or attendance register, or whatever other documents there are relating to children.)

Hostesses
Like foster people, the hostesses generally work behind the scenes, providing refreshments before or after the service. It would be good to draw attention to them occasionally.

Servers
In churches which have servers, their role is clearly defined. The leader might mention them by name at some point in the commentary.

Have you thought . . . of using girls as servers? If care, loyalty and reverence are the qualifications for servers, girls often out-do the boys in these characteristics. The new cassock-alb is a unisex garment and looks well on both boys and girls.

Sidesmen/Stewards
It is often assumed that the family service is the children's show, and that they should therefore take over all (or most of) the duties normally done by the adults. If the service is to be truly integrated worship, then this is not a good idea. A fair balance must be sought in the carrying out of the usual duties so that the church's officers are not displaced and the children learn to respect the duties of others. If possible, children should be clearly under the control of the existing officers, and used as helpers when this is practicable. The aim is to give the children a chance to share in the simple responsibilities such as collecting, giving out hymn books, etc. without displacing the adults. We want to avoid any idea of the all-age act of worship being a 'children's service' or a 'junior church'.

Have you thought . . . of inviting a family to undertake sidesmen's duties on a particular Sunday?

Section 4. The Address or Sermon

The address at an all-age service needs careful preparation and imaginative and sensitive handling. There should be a simple clear aim, preferably one point which can be illustrated and developed in ways which will appeal to young children, to the teenagers, and also to the adults. As we also have to bear in mind the needs of both regular churchgoers and occasional visitors, this is a really tall order!

During an address there are two things happening simultaneously. Someone is talking *and* a group is listening. Anyone can get up and talk; but it is quite another thing to enable people to listen. There is a need to be absolutely practical. Consider the acoustics of the building; there may be an echo, or a chancel arch which distorts or takes away the sound. It may be that the building needs amplification equipment. If so, let it be properly adjusted beforehand to suit a particular speaker.

The diction and delivery must suit the building. A golden rule is to *speak slowly* and enunciate clearly, especially emphasising consonant sounds. However brilliant the speaker may be, if he cannot be heard easily the people will not listen.

A pitfall which must be avoided at all costs, especially if there are young people present, is the temptation to talk down to the children. They hate it and often react strongly against any speaker who puts on a 'talking-to-the-children' voice. Young people are quick to see through any cant or hypocrisy. They respond readily to the approach which is natural and genuine; and they like a challenge. Far better a point which makes them reach out than one which in their minds is dismissed as babyish.

Mannerisms can be irritating and off-putting to those trying to listen. A good, firm deliberate gesture, or a look or a movement may enhance a point. Body language is very important in communication; but the unconscious and irritating habit only distracts. Another practical hint is to make previous arrangements with sidesmen or stewards to encourage the congregation to sit together in the front seats. This is especially important for folk who may be slightly deaf. One comment to a preacher from an old lady was: 'I did so much enjoy your sermon, Vicar—I didn't hear a word!'

The preacher needs to think about where he should stand during the address. Much will depend on the building, on the occasion, or on the speaker himself. Sometimes the pulpit may be the right place: there is somewhere for your notes, something to hold on to, and (as one nervous curate commented) something to hide your tottering knees! There is also the advantage and perhaps the authority which comes from being raised up. If, however, you wish to establish a more informal atmosphere and try to involve the congregation in the sermon, it is easier to do this on a level with them, from the centre of the chancel or altar steps.

A congregation is much more likely to pay attention to what you say if you look straight at individuals when you make your points. You can then get a kind of 'feed-back' from their expressions, their smiles or even their looks of disapproval, and it is possible with experience to make quick adjustments to suit the mood of the congregation. Again this is easier if you are not tied to one particular spot, and able to move about the congregation in order, perhaps, to receive answers from children, or to make sure that everyone can see a particular aid you are using.

Another practical point: if you do need notes, make sure they are neatly and clearly written out on cards or small pieces of paper if there is no stand to put them on. A carefully-prepared talk will soon be ruined if papers flutter about or if you lose your place.

It is very important that the sermon should be relevant to the needs of the people who are in church. It is no good being very sophisticated and deeply theological if the majority of the people just don't know what you are talking about. Avoid your latest theological hobby-horse (if you have one): but if you really feel moved to comment on a current theological issue, perhaps one aired on television or in the press, do so only if you know that there are people in the congregation who really want to hear more about it. It is a good idea to have the planning group suggest topics for the address, issues which people need to think about, or aspects of the faith which the newcomers and children ought to know.

In *The Paradox of Worship* Michael Perry wrote: 'The sermon is a declaration of the counsel or gospel of God to a particular congregation in a particular place at a particular period in its history, and if it is a good sermon, it will bear signs of that "earthing". The minister may be aware of what *he* wants to say, but it may be that the congregation has different needs from the ones he imagines. The theology may be too abstract for them. They may need milk instead of meat. The things that are bothering him may not be the things which are bothering them—as an African layman once said of his pastor: "He's always scratching me where I don't itch".' (p.55)

Putting it Over
Having decided on a topic which you know is relevant, and having in mind a single and clear aim, there are many different ways of putting the message across apart from just speaking it to a passive audience. In all-age worship, aim to try to elicit some response which will stimulate growth.

Questioning
Start with the younger people; they are likely to be less inhibited and they are often keen to answer the searching question. Be prepared to be surprised and amused by some of the answers. During a Christmas sermon an imaginative preacher used a real dog in a real manger. 'And what does a dog do in a manger?' he asked, warming to his theme. 'He makes a mess!' came the immediate reply! Good questioning, however, does engage the congregation and young people often have insights which are really profound. 'Why did God create mankind?' asked one leader. 'Because he likes company', was the thought-provoking reply.

Story
Most people listen to stories, and they can be a most effective way of communicating. Jesus was a master in the art of story-telling, as the parables recorded in the Gospels amply demonstrate. There are many books of stories, but perhaps the best way is to make your own collection—whenever you hear a good story, record it. It is always more effective when a story is told rather than read. Make it your own and your hearers will respond. The story or illustration must be relevant to the general aim; it is of little use if people enjoy and remember the story without seeing any connection with the theme of the sermon.

Music
Have you ever thought of encouraging the congregation to think about the words of a hymn, and use that as the basis of an address? It may be an excellent opportunity to teach a new hymn. You will prepare this, of course, by seeking the co-operation of the organist and choir; they are often pleased to be asked and may perhaps be called upon to help

Whenever you hear a good story, record it . . .

with the presentation. Another way of using music is to play a recording of a well-known song (the Top Twenty can often provide a suitable one) and use that as a starter for a talk.

Drama

The use of drama in church has an advantage of involving more people. It can be a most thought-provoking way of making a point. A short play could be prepared for a particular service. It must be well-rehearsed and presented in such a way that it can be clearly seen and heard by everyone. Alternatively, drama could be quite spontaneous. Young people can be invited from the congregation and asked to do a mime or a role-play to illustrate a particular point. The best age for this is up to 12 years; adolescents are often shy and self-conscious and should not be asked unless you know they would be happy to take part. There may be one or two willing adults who would not mind helping out.

Pictures and posters

There are some excellent posters available today, some with imaginative captions. They can occasionally be used to reinforce a point or make people think, and young people are often very pleased to be asked to hold up a picture or wander round the church with it.

Projectors

Filmstrips and slides abound on all kinds of religious topics, and their use makes a stimulating alternative to the usual sermon. There may be photographic expertise available to enable you to make up a collection of home-produced slides for a family service, perhaps with a tape-recorded commentary as well. Unless you can black out the church, a back-projection screen will be needed. Make sure the equipment works properly and that the operator knows thoroughly what he is doing!

Visual aids

It is important that the aids which are used do make a serious contribution, and really help people to concentrate on the aim of the sermon. Simple, sometimes quite unusual objects can be pressed into service as visual aids: for instance, one preacher has used a collection of teddy bears, giving them each a particular character and then developing a story about them (see page 83). He found that people quite naturally identified with one or other of the characters in a way they would not have done if he had spoken to them 'straight'. In using visual aids, it is important that the preacher should be master of the aid, and not the other way round!

Movement

As we have said above, the preacher may wish to move about the congregation during the address for some particular purpose such as questioning or handing something out. It may also be possible to have some of the young people moving about to find something out. Young children cannot be expected to sit still for very long. For example, at Easter, the children in one congregation were encouraged to go to the Easter Garden during the service to discover one thing about it. This they were able to tell their parents back in the pews. Thus they became in their own right witnesses to the Resurrection, and it was the answers which the *parents* gave which formed the basis of the address.

Another quite inspiring way of using movement is to prepare a liturgical dance. Our worship is often rather too sedentary, and once folk have broken through the barrier of English reserve they can sometimes be liberated and renewed in a most refreshing way by joining in an activity in which they use their bodies to express the theme of the worship.

Dialogue
Another interesting way of presenting the address or sermon is by using two people to put opposing views, rather like a debate, either by inviting two prominent local people, or using members of the congregation who have been carefully prepared. This method stimulates people's thinking about issues which may be controversial. A summing up by a third party is generally needed. The 'interview' technique can also be used to effect, as in one church where, using this method, a group of young people recently returned from a pilgrimage to Taizé in France were able to share their experiences with the rest of the congregation.

Humour
Among the most popular figures in the world of entertainment is the comedian. It is worth noting that comedians deal very effectively with quite serious topics because they show up the absurdity and pomposity of much that goes on in society. Humour can be a most useful way of communicating, and one which appeals to every age. It is good to notice that people are beginning to feel much less inhibited about laughing in church. Laughter is one of God's greatest gifts to us, because it helps to dispel illusions.

The main function of the address at a family service should be, in preaching the Gospel, to stimulate growth. Give each child, each adolescent and each adult something to think about and to pray about so that they can respond wholeheartedly. The address should never concentrate so much on one group in the congregation that you lose touch with the others, so do not assume that it has to be aimed primarily at the children. It is possible, by directing your remarks carefully and choosing your vocabulary with equal care, to say something relevant for every age-group and for every stage of spiritual development.

It is important for the preacher to remember that the sermon is presented in the name of God. It is one way in which God speaks to us, through his Holy Spirit. Worship is God's business, an activity which he has invited us to share. Part of the preparation should be to pray that God will use you in the way he wants, to communicate the Gospel and to be an effective witness. It is heartening to know that the Holy Spirit often does work when we think we have failed.

Section 5. Prayers

The leader responsible for the prayers in an all-age service needs an approach which is flexible, adaptable, and capable of variety. It needs to be emphasised that the set forms of prayer in most prayer books have only a limited value in the context of family worship. Even the more adaptable forms of Series 2 and 3 and the collections of contemporary prayers need to be treated very freely if they are used.

In all-age worship, the average power of concentration of the congregation is on the low side. Therefore, prayer-time should be brief. It is not necessary to include, every Sunday, the whole of local and national and international affairs of Church and State. It is not necessary even to run through every clause of the set intercession in the service book.

There is a power about the printed word which impels some people to assume that what is printed must be used. In fact, leaders in congregational prayer for all-age worship must be ready to break away from the rigidities of the printed word, even of home-produced duplicated orders of service. It is far better to be selective, relevant, and *brief*. Probably three or four concerns are sufficient for any one prayer episode. The principle of compensation could apply here: the longer the hymns, or sermon, or notices, the shorter the prayers, so that the overall length of the service remains the same, preferably not more than one hour.

Formal Prayers

Familiar prayers
Set liturgical prayers, and other well-known prayers have their place in all-age worship, whether they are recited by the leader on behalf of the congregation, or whether they are read or said 'in chorus' by everybody. It is a mistake to try and simplify the language in such prayers. They are common property, and have a cumulative effect by their repetition. They contain material which needs to be expounded in the course of the church's education programme, so bit by bit worshippers assimilate them and make them their own.

Included in such prayers are: The Lord's Prayer, the Eucharistic Thanksgiving, Collects for Morning and Evening Prayer, The Grace, and such famous prayers as the prayers of St Richard, St Teresa, St Ignatius, the General Thanksgiving, the Prayer of St Francis, and many others.

Collects

It is helpful to an all-age congregation if Collects and other short, formal prayers are prefixed by a very short introduction: e.g. 'In the Collect for Ash Wednesday, we hear about God's mercy and forgiveness'. If possible, include in the introduction one or two words which will come in the prayer.

Litanies and Responses

These need to be short, and clear directions must be given: e.g. if the sentences are in the service book or written out, refer to the people's part—'We say the sentences on page . . .: will you please say the answers' (or 'will you please say the sentences marked "people"'). If the people have not got a copy, the litany form can be used on occasions, with the instruction 'When I say, "Lord, in your mercy", you reply, "Hear our prayer".' N.B. It is *not* sufficient to say 'After each sentence will you say "Hear our prayers, O Lord"'—because the congregation cannot concentrate on the prayers if they are always wondering when to come in with their part.

Informal Prayers

Extempore

This is the most difficult form of public prayer to use properly, although if it is well done, there is no better form for all-age worship. The leader using extempore prayer should bear in mind the following points:—

Extempore prayer used in a church service must not be allowed to become too personal. The leader must be constantly aware that he is engaging in public, liturgical prayer, and this is not the same as praying aloud in a small house-group or meeting.

It is not necessary to be visible, but wherever he stands he must be audible. The words he chooses must be clear, precise, and simple without being childish. He should avoid the use of abstract words as far as possible—e.g. NOT 'We do thank you for our creation and preservation', BUT—'Thank you, God our Father, for making us, thank you for giving us the world to live in, and thank you for taking care of us.'

Mannerisms are usually associated with actions, but mannerisms of voice are just as important to look out for, and can be equally distracting:

e.g. the use of certain unnecessary words like 'do' 'We *do* ask you to bless . . .' or 'We *do* thank you for . . .' (Just say, 'Please bless . . .', 'Thank you for . . .'). The 'parsonical' or 'talking to God' voice is both unnecessary and irritating, as is the 'talking-to-the-children' voice. To eliminate this, tape-recorders are helpful; honest parishioners even more so!

It is better to have one prayer for one idea, i.e. a 'thank-you' prayer followed by a 'please' prayer, rather than to put the two altogether in one long prayer. Sentences should be short, and the leader needs to know where he is going in order to avoid getting tangled up (like the inexperienced minister who once found himself at the end of such a long and involved sentence that he had to pause and then continue— 'paradoxical though it may seem to thee, O Lord').

A studied earnestness is the worst fault in extempore praying (as in other kinds too). The leader must be sincere enough to make the prayer his own, natural enough to be able to pray without affectation, and yet completely aware of the whole congregation whose prayerful thoughts he is trying to guide. Such expertise only comes with practice and experience.

In view of the foregoing remarks, it is obviously desirable to train lay people (and clergy too!) in the art of leading extempore prayer. This can best be done by getting them to write out their own prayers first, and read them from the manuscript, until they are confident enough to manage without.

Say after me
This is quite a useful form of praying, provided that it isn't used too often, because some adults will consider it an insult to their intelligence. The remarks (above) on brevity, clarity and audibility will apply here. Sentences must be broken up into short sections which make sense in themselves, so that it is not too much strain on the memory. Clear directions must be given: 'Say these words after me.' (Not as one theological student once said: 'I want you to repeat after me, phrase by phrase . . .'—and was then stopped in his tracks by the children responding—'Phrase by phrase.')

Musical prayer
A specific choir or solo item may be prepared and used as a 'listening' prayer for the congregation. If the words are significant (sometimes they are subordinate to the music) it is helpful for the congregation to

have a copy or to see them projected or written up. A short instrumental solo or organ voluntary is often useful as a prelude to prayers. Alternatively, the congregation could be asked to use a hymn or song as a prayer, being led quite informally into unaccompanied singing. Make sure the hymn *is* a prayer: e.g. 'There is a green hill far away' (AM rev. 214) is not a prayer, but 'O dearest Lord, thy sacred head' (AM rev. 436) is a prayer. Of the modern songs, 'Kum ba ya' is an obvious choice for an intercessory prayer, provided it is prefaced by some introductory remarks e.g. 'When we sing, "Someone's crying, Lord"—we shall be thinking about Mrs X who is ill, or sick children' etc.

Lists
It is sometimes useful to collect names for intercession from the congregation before the service begins. It is best if these are written up on a board large enough for everyone to see. The names can either be mentioned out loud during prayers, or made the object of silent prayer. Large clear pictures or slides can be similarly used as visual aids to prayer. The leader could also use on occasions last night's paper as a starting point. 'I'm reading here about a child who was run over yesterday. She's called Joy. Let's say a prayer for her, and for her Mum and Dad.' It is often helpful to have an intercession board at the back of the church which can be referred to.

Use of silence
Traditional worshippers are sometimes upset that there is little or no opportunity for quiet devotions at a family service. In general, all-age worship is not conducive to this type of praying, and opportunity needs to be given for it in church at other times: the 8 o'clock Communion, the evening service, or during the week. The importance of quiet prayer needs to be referred to on occasions in the family service, with notices given out as to what provision is made for it in the church's total programme. Having said that, it is often possible in a family service to achieve a sense of quiet in the prayers without actually attempting to force a silence, simply by making short pauses at the ends of sentences. The leader needs to adopt a relaxed and unhurried style, trying to avoid the current neurosis which seeks to fill every space with noise. If there is an opportunity for a spot of real quiet during the course of a family service, it is a good idea to grasp it. It is better to refer to this as a 'Short time of quiet', rather than silence. It is probably as well for the leader to suggest what the congregation does with it: e.g. 'Pray quietly for someone you know . . . your home and family . . . a friend . . . a sick person.' Or—'Listen to Jesus speaking these words in your mind—I am

with you always' (or use some other short quotation). However, insensitivity to local conditions could make nonsense of this exercise; for instance, when the leader says 'We will now have a few moments of silent prayer', apparently oblivious of the squawking infant at the back, or the motor-bike enthusiast in the garage opposite the church door. If the battle is lost before you start, admit it, and either get everyone to join in a familiar prayer they know, or one they can read together, or just sing or say a well-known hymn instead.

Some Practical Suggestions for Prayer Leaders

Posture

Be sensitive to the wide variety of congregational needs. Sitting or standing may sometimes be the best posture for prayer. Kneeling should be used sparingly if at all, and always with an escape clause: i.e. 'Please feel free to sit or kneel for the prayers'. The main reason for this is that young children may make a considerable disturbance when trying to kneel at the very moment when you want to be as calm as possible. In addition, they tend to get lost behind (or even under) the pews or chairs and then contract out of the service altogether until the prayers are over. It might be a good idea for the leader to ask himself the question 'Why do we kneel?' And don't forget the needs of the older people.

They tend to get lost . . .

Many voices

Modern forms of prayer sometimes seem to lend themselves to dividing up amongst several people; e.g. the Intercessions in Series 3. This may be effective in a school service, but it is difficult to do successfully in church. A mixed congregation can concentrate better with one voice than with many. There may be special occasions when several people could lead the prayers but this should be the exception rather than the rule.

Relevant and realistic

Phrases like—'Let us pray for all the people in Africa'—are not very helpful. On the whole, it is better to specify than to generalise in prayer, or at least to include specific people or concerns within the general topic, e.g. 'We ask you, Lord, to bless the people suffering as a result of the earthquake. We have seen their pictures on our television sets. Bless and heal the children we have seen; help the rescue workers and give them courage and strength, especially the doctors short of sleep. Help us to remember to give what we can to the Christian Aid Appeal, so that we can help too, for Jesus's sake.'

Children's own prayers

Left on their own, children's prayers, however delightful in their naïveté, can become rather too slight for a congregation in which adults are participating. A good mix of both children's and adults' prayers should be aimed at.

Eyes closed?

It is quite possible to pray with eyes open, and sometimes it is worth making a point of this in the family service. Usually it is best if the open eyes are directed somewhere, on to a cross or picture as a focus of attention.

Guided meditation

There may be someone who can reproduce the idea found in Michel Quoist's books, that of meditating aloud on a single object or concern. This is a good way to add variety in praying, but it needs to be used with restraint; it can be overdone.

Note

As with the use of illustrations in a sermon, it is sometimes possible to 'lose' a section of the congregation by suggesting a prayer theme which is too 'highly-charged'; if, for instance, there are a fair number of boys in the congregation, it would be unwise to pray for FA Cup teams!

PART THREE—IN PREPARATION

page

Section 1. Planning and Assessing

We recognise that churches differ widely in their resources and potential. In some, it may be difficult to find enough jobs to suit all the people who may want to be involved, whereas in others the problem may well be to find enough people to do the jobs! The following illustrations assume that a reasonable number of people would be found to help plan and assess family worship. A church with limited lay resources will need to modify the various suggestions to fit its own situation.

This section is in two parts. Part A suggests a way of planning and assessing an all-age worship programme for a whole year. Part B contains an account of how the detailed planning for a family service evolved within a small parish in Cheshire.

Part A
1. Appoint your team for long-term planning.
2. Sub-divide into groups (detail planners) for a particular service or series of services.

1. The long-term planners
  The clergy
  Representatives of:-
    Sunday School
    Other children's organisations
    Youth Work
    Adult education
    P.C.C.

The group will probably need to meet only two or three times a year to make outline plans for the whole of the twelve months. Early September, January and after Easter are recommended as convenient times at which to make long-term plans.

First of all, it is a good idea to deal with the major festivals within the period, and take a decision whether this year they are going to be treated in isolation, or if a theme is to be planned culminating in the festival. Much will depend on the frequency of the family services. If they are weekly, the September meeting might decide:-
(a) what is to happen at Harvest, All Saints-tide, Advent and Christmas

(b) what themes will be followed in the intervening weeks

(c) the allocation of leaders to be responsible for this series of services.

A long-term plan for *weekly* family services from September to the end of the year might be:-

September Main Theme: Looking forward to the Harvest.

first Sunday — Harvest of the Land.

second Sunday — Harvest Overseas.

third Sunday — Harvest of the Sea.

fourth Sunday — Harvest Festival.

If there are five Sundays in September, the Harvest of Industry could be included. In a city parish this would in any case probably take preference over the Harvest of the Land.

October Main Theme: 'For all the Saints'

first Sunday — St Francis (4th October)—a saint who cared for animals and birds. Link with work of Blue Cross Society, RSPCA, etc.

second Sunday — St Stephen (whose feast is often overlooked as it is so near to Christmas). The first Christian martyr — influenced Saul's conversion. Link with contemporary martyrs.

third Sunday — St Luke (18th October)—faithful companion of Paul. Patron saint of physicians. Importance of the Healing Ministry, dedication of medical staff.

fourth Sunday — Mother Teresa of Calcutta—a practical saint who cares for outcasts today.

November

first Sunday — Service for All Saints-tide based on the October services.

As Remembrance Sunday is observed in most churches at this time, a decision has to be taken by the planning group regarding the remainder of the Sundays in November. The theme of 'Saints' could be extended with Martin of Tours (11th November), St Cecilia (22nd November) and St Andrew (30th November), with St Nicholas (6th December) an obvious choice for the first Sunday in December when many parishes have Christingle or Toy services.

If, however, the planning group feels that the All Saints-tide service should conclude this particular theme, then there is still a useful period left in which to work through a pre-Advent and Advent course. Many

58

parishes find the two *Share the Word* books (CIO), *Live, Learn and Worship* (CIO) and the *Partners in Learning* series (NCEC) invaluable sources for new ideas and fresh approaches. Like the new lectionary, they begin at the Fifth Sunday before Advent.

In parishes where family services are held *once a month*, the long-term planners have the problem of achieving some kind of continuity. A month is a long time for a child's memory to span, and many adults would admit to similar problems! Where the monthly family service is the only occasion when instruction is given to the children, it becomes vitally important that the best use is made of the time available and that the teaching is structured rather than haphazard. In order to achieve this continuity and sense of purpose, it is a very good idea to have an overall theme going from month to month, although each family service would be complete in itself.

Thus, the long-term plan for a monthly family service from January to May/June might be as follows:-

Theme: Prayer.
Link Activity: The hand of prayer.

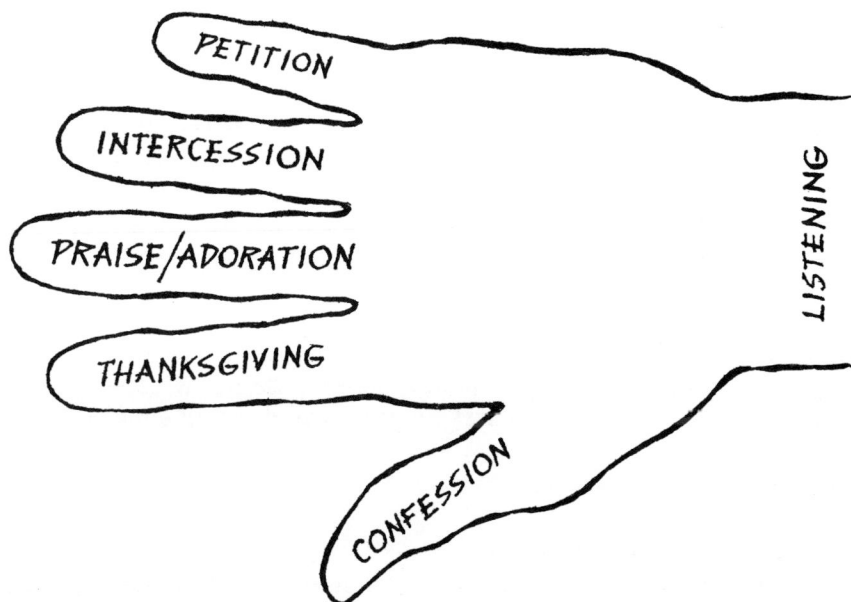

You will need: One large copy of a hand for display in church; sufficient paper, felt pens etc. for children to make one 'hand' each; prayer folders for both children and adults in which to keep appropriate prayer cards from each of the services.

This idea is an adaptation of the well-tried activity which illustrates the different aspects of worship.

January: Adoration with the Wise Men.

February: Confession—beginning of Lent.

March: Thanksgiving (if mid-Lent—for Mothers, Mother Church etc.)

April: Intercession.

May: Petition (Rogationtide)

These monthly topics could be interchanged, depending on when Easter falls. If a sixth subject is required, 'Listening' could be added in June. The large chart would be filled in each month with the appropriate word and the children would make the necessary addition to their 'hands'. Older children and adults could be given folders into which they could stick copies of prayers appropriate to the day's theme. Considerable thought would need to be given to the choice of these prayers and it would be a very worthwhile exercise in adult education to call a separate meeting to discuss this question. It is well known that many adults fail to grow up in their prayer-life and this would be an excellent opportunity to introduce good contemporary prayers as well as the classics of St Teresa, St Richard and Ignatius Loyola and others.

In many churches there is a Sunday school or similar activity for the instruction of the children in the weeks between the family services. In this kind of situation it is advantageous to plan the children's work with a view to a presentation in church of the project in which they have been involved. The lesson courses mentioned earlier are very helpful here.

Different age-groups could take the responsibility for one service each, beginning with the younger children, as they do not usually need as much time to explore a theme as do juniors and young seniors.

From Easter to Trinitytide, the long-term plan for this kind of situation could be:-

Overall theme: Recreation.

May (Presentation by the under-sevens) Holidays—the joys of the sea-side etc. Importance of holidays—need for renewal.

June (Presentation by junior children) Re-creation—a new start. e.g. new classes, new schools, 'going up', links with Ascensiontide and Whitsunday—the new start for the disciples.

July (Presentation by older juniors/young seniors) St Paul's new start—his conversion, his missionary journeys.

2. The detail planners

Once the long-term plans have been decided, it is necessary to appoint leaders to be responsible for particular Sundays or groups of Sundays. They in turn choose their team and it is at this stage that many more people become involved. Decisions have to be taken regarding the actual content of the service; hymns, prayers and readings chosen and rehearsed. Any visual aids or special sound effects need preparing and checking. If any new musical items have been selected it is diplomatic to give the organist and choir as much advance warning as possible.

The leaders must co-ordinate the work of their own team and it is a great advantage when recruiting help if it is shown that not every member of the team needs to be on duty every week. Many busy lay people cannot commit themselves to helping on a regular basis, but are prepared to give their time and skill for limited periods. If several teams are organised in this way, some variety of thought and presentation is ensured, more people become involved and no one group has a monopoly. The teams who are 'fallow' will no doubt take a keen interest in the approach of the current presenter and all will have the chance to be learning from each other.

Evaluation

After taking a family service, it should be quite natural for the leader to look for comment from some of the congregation. Even adverse criticism is better than total silence! Best of all is a considered evaluation from a group of people representative of the general congregation. This could take the form of a de-briefing session of the group which was drawn together to plan the event. Otherwise, some of the other people involved in the church's work might be approached; they could be expected to give a more objective analysis than those actually involved in the planning.

The underlying questions that should be in the minds of anyone assessing the effectiveness of a service are whether or not they were in God's presence, whether the Good News was proclaimed and some response to it sought, explicitly or implicitly, from the congregation. By making this kind of assessment, it should be possible to avoid the type

E

of family service in which all kinds of things were going on, everyone enjoyed it, and yet nothing happened!

Bearing this in mind, there are some practical points with respect to each service which could be considered by those evaluating:-
  (a) length:
      if too long, what could have been omitted with least damage to the theme? if too short, was anything important missing?
  (b) interest and attention:
      was it sustained? if not, when did it begin to wander? was the weakness in the content or the delivery?
  (c) overall response:
      was the message received?
  (d) was it a happy occasion?
  (e) were there enough helpers?
  (f) was the new material effective? If so could it be adapted for another occasion—and how soon?
  (g) any problems?
Any criticism or comment must be positive with the purpose of leading to improvements next time. It must be honest, but not unkind, helpful but not destructive. It must always be remembered that it takes courage to invite criticism and more courage to accept it in the right spirit.

One of the advantages of having a group to assess any particular service is that critics are more likely to make their comments to people other than the leader, particularly if they have not been impressed by what went on. The group members receiving criticisms of this kind can then act as buffers and if necessary do a little tactful re-phrasing at the evaluation meeting. A further advantage of this indirect 'feedback' is that it is likely to be more candid and worthy of notice than the customary 'nice sermon, Vicar' type of remark that some people find obligatory at the church door.

Part B

An account of how a family service was planned and assessed in a Cheshire parish church.

The parish is semi-rural with a population of about 2,000. The church is staffed by a vicar and a lay-reader. The weekly pattern of worship is 8.30 a.m. Holy Communion, 10 a.m. Family Eucharist and 6.30 p.m

Evensong. There is a Sunday School at 11.15 a.m. in the day-school building, about ten minutes' walk from the church.

The Church Council set up a worship committee which received the complaint that the Family Eucharist was not meeting the needs of the children, who were bored, nor of the adults, who were distracted by the bored children. As an experiment, it was decided to allocate the first Sunday in each month to various lay people who were given a free hand to experiment, within the framework of Series 3 Holy Communion, in presenting an act of worship in which all age-groups could participate. One of the committee, a lecturer in a College of Education, undertook to start the ball rolling. Other people invited to keep it moving included the Parochial Reader, the lady in charge of overseas work, a primary school teacher, and the Vicar himself. These people could call on others to help and were responsible for co-ordinating the work of their own small teams.

The first leader, a keen student of the Bible, decided to make his new approach through the Epistle for the Sunday, which happened to be Philemon. Instead of reading it in the customary way, he narrated it as a story with the aid of large pictures which had been prepared by his wife who teaches Art.

He began with a picture of a Roman soldier and one of Paul, thus setting the scene of the apostle in his prison cell. The next two pictures of Onesimus the runaway slave and Philemon his master were brought to life as the congregation were directed to clues in the text about their behaviour. The message of the need to face up to one's faults, then do something practical to make amends, was simple enough for the children to grasp as it concerned the real people they had met through the illustrations. At the same time it gave the adults new insight into that particular epistle and an incentive to go home and read it again for themselves.

The next 'first Sunday' was mid-Lent and the responsibility of the primary school teacher. She was confronted with the challenge of Mothering Sunday. All the usual approaches (such as gifts of flowers, cards, simnel cake) had been tried on previous occasions. Clearly a new one was needed involving as many of the congregation as possible. Inspiration was found in the book *Our Mum* by David Yates (CIO) which gives five themes for family services especially for Mothering Sunday. One of the suggestions given was to hold a communal quiz on 'what makes a happy home'.

It was decided to extend this idea and make it the central theme emphasising the importance of happy family life rather than concentrating solely on Mum. *Our Mum* also furnished the idea of lighting a Sabbath Candle at the beginning of the service. It was lit by the wife of the churchwarden as this couple had recently celebrated their golden wedding; this fact was mentioned and appropriate congratulations given from their church family. The book also provided the reading from 'A Wedding Sermon from a Prison Cell' by Dietrich Bonhoeffer, and the hymn 'Every child has a Mother'. As this was new to everyone, the local primary school was asked if they would practise it with the children.

One of the special cards published by the Mothers' Union was chosen to be given to the children and the help of the Enrolling Member was enlisted in purchasing a supply of these cards. The Branch was invited to attend the service and to carry their banner in the opening procession which they were pleased to do on this occasion, even though most of their members normally attend the 8.30 or 6.30 services. A family was invited to carry the bread, the wine and the cards in the offertory procession.

The following people were involved before the Sunday:-

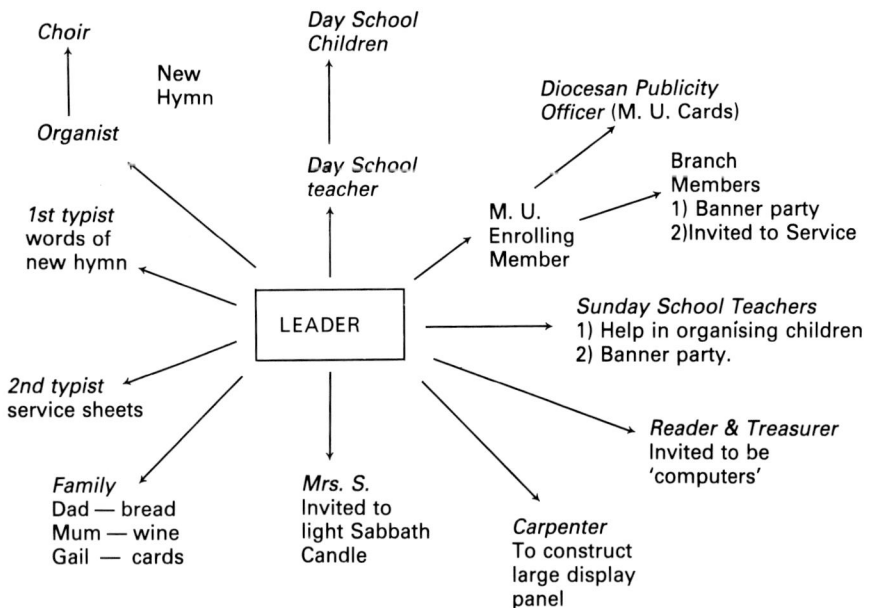

Choir

Organist

New
Hymn

Day School
Children

Day School
teacher

Diocesan Publicity
Officer (M. U. Cards)

Branch
Members
1) Banner party
2)Invited to Service

1st typist
words of
new hymn

M. U.
Enrolling
Member

LEADER

Sunday School Teachers
1) Help in organising children
2) Banner party.

2nd typist
service sheets

Reader & Treasurer
Invited to be
'computers'

Family
Dad — bread
Mum — wine
Gail — cards

Mrs. S.
Invited to
light Sabbath
Candle

Carpenter
To construct
large display
panel

Had time permitted it would have been pleasant and helpful if this group had met together over coffee to have the plans for the service explained to them. As it happened, shortage of time meant that the leader saw each of them in turn. This in itself had its value as it involved giving a direct invitation rather than a general one to the individuals or groups involved.

In addition to visiting these people, the leader had certain visual aids to prepare, namely, a giant-size cereal packet and ten large cards on which were written the captions shown below (page 66) (These could have been made by a group of juniors or young seniors, giving rise to a discussion about what to include in the 'Ask the Family' competition).

A giant-size cereal packet . . .

The outline of the service was as follows:-
Procession—with Sunday School, M.U., Guides and Banners.
Welcome and candle-lighting ceremony
(brief explanation of the Jewish custom with the aid of Nelson picture B.8. 'The Holy Family at Table').

Prayer—said by all mothers, god-mothers and grandmothers. 'Blessed are you, Lord God of all creation. You have called us to live together in love. Make our homes and families your dwelling place and bless us as we celebrate this holy day'.
Reading—a letter from prison by Dietrich Bonhoeffer. (The congregation was invited to listen to what he wrote about a home).

Liturgical Game—Ask the Family. A giant-sized carton of 'Weetibangs' was displayed bearing a competition on its side: 'What do you think makes a happy home?' Ten captions were to be put in order of precedence. These were discussed briefly in turn before being displayed in random order on a large board. They included obvious statements like 'enough to eat', those requiring more thought such as 'sharing things we enjoy' and 'sharing things we don't enjoy' (i.e. disappointments, sorrows, disgrace) and red-herrings like 'colour TV' and 'two cars'.

When the ten captions were on the board the congregation were invited to enter the competition as families. One child from each group came for an entry form and a pencil, and five minutes were allowed in which to discuss and allocate the captions into their order of precedence. The entry forms looked like this:

What makes a happy home?
Please put in order of precedence:

Putting up with each other
Affection
Two cars
Discipline and self-control
Enough to eat
Lots of money
Sharing things we enjoy
Sharing things we don't enjoy
Colour TV
Listening to each other

Where members of the congregation were not in family units they were asked to become 'pew families' and fill in a form with their immediate neighbours. The Guides who were on parade were asked to work in sixes, three from one pew turning round to work with the three behind them. Tiny children were given outline pictures of their home and the church to colour in with large wax crayons. (The Sunday school staff supervised their distribution.) Members of the choir were invited to rejoin their own families or to work as a choir family.

The next five minutes were crucial. Would the idea work or would it flop? Fortunately, it worked! That busy hum signifying absorbed concentration was heard throughout the church. A bell was rung to mark the end of the five minutes and the papers were collected by the Guides. It was announced that they would be processed by our own computer and the results given out later.

The service then continued with the special hymn for Mothering Sunday. Appropriate prayers followed, then the Series 3 order for Holy Communion was resumed from the Offertory. The 'computers' (two lay people previously selected) worked out of sight and completed their task before the Consecration. This enabled the leader to re-arrange the ten captions on the board when she had received Communion. This gave the large congregation something to think about as they waited during the administration of Communion. While this provoked some further discussion in the family groups it was done quietly and did not appear to disturb the other people.

By the time Communion was over, the ten captions were in order of preference and it was only necessary for the leader to make brief closing remarks; the results spoke for themselves:

1.	Affection	272
2.	Listening to each other	209
3.	Discipline and self-control	183
4.	Sharing things we don't enjoy	182
5.	Putting up with each other	181
6.	Sharing things we enjoy	181
7.	Enough to eat	138
8.	Lots of money	52
9.	Colour TV	39
10.	Two cars	26

After the service, three kinds of evaluation took place:

1. *The immediate reaction* of
(a) the leader—'it has worked'

(b) the congregation, several of whom went out of their way to say thank you for the careful preparation.

2. *The indirect feedback* through the Lay Reader and the Worship Group. This was particularly valuable as it was more likely to be honest than the conventionally polite remarks made to the leader herself.

3. *A discussion* among some of the Education Team regarding the value of the event. The verdict was that it had been a great success with every age-group within the congregation and was an idea that could be used again at some future occasion. One suggestion was to make the subject for the next 'Ask the Family' quiz, 'What makes a good Sunday School'? with separate entry forms for the parents and the children. The results of this competition could then be used by the team planning the educational programme in the parish.

Section 2. The Building

The remarks on liturgy in Part One chapter two contain some thoughts about the fact that leaders of family worship need to take a fresh look at the church building. This small section includes a few practical points in relation to the building which were not mentioned in that chapter.

It may be, for instance, that you are thinking of some modification to the building with family worship in mind. Obviously a careful study needs to be made by the Church Council, working together with the appropriate church authorities, and preferably in consultation with an architect who has some experience in all-age worship. There would not be much point in going into great detail here about the possibilities for re-arrangement in old churches; circumstances vary so widely. We would recommend, however, that two basic principles should be grasped by anyone responsible for such re-arrangement (and this goes for the provision of new buildings too); these are SPACE AND FLEXIBILITY.

Space
Nothing is more depressing than empty pews or chairs; but a sense of space makes for a feeling of liberation and joy. Family services require, above all else, opportunity for *meeting* and *movement*, and space is needed to allow for this. One obvious area for the provision of space is at or near the entrance, but other spacious areas are much to be desired so that display and/or movement can be allowed for as part of the service.

Flexibility
The serried ranks of timber in most of our Victorianised churches say more about patterns of conventional behaviour than about liturgical excellence. It is so much more useful (and meaningful) if seating can be adaptable and capable of re-arrangement to suit different occasions and numbers of people. This becomes obvious if the family service is to include any kind of drama or display, or if numbers of worshippers are expected to be very much more or less than the normal seating provides for.

F

Atmosphere

We often hear about the 'atmosphere' of a church, particularly of an ancient church. This indefinable quality about a place or building has something to do with its location and use and the amount of prayer and worship that has been taking place there. Whatever it is, atmosphere reminds us that first impressions are very important. In this respect, no amount of atmosphere will compensate for a church which is not kept clean, tidy and well-cared-for. So please pay attention to the following:

Notice-boards

See that these are up-to-date and tidy, with attractive display material. There are all kinds of good posters available these days. With a little imagination, posters can be produced locally (by a school perhaps) to illustrate a particular theme. Inside the church, colourful displays can be set up by various parish groups in turn. One idea is to use photographs to illustrate aspects of church or parish life; people love to see themselves and their friends on a notice-board, and the groups crowding round give an immediate sense of togetherness which is what all-age worship is partly about.

Flowers

Most of our churches excel in flower arrangements, but sometimes the dead ones still get left behind.

Have you ever thought . . . when flowers are expensive, of befriending your local undertaker? He is often asked by relatives of the deceased for suggestions as to what can be done with funeral flowers after the service! Remember, though, to strip them of all funeral wrappings, etc. so that a carefully-disguised re-arrangement can be effected.

Books, clothes etc.

Hymn and prayer books should be neatly stored or arranged, and always aim to keep the choir robes, servers' garments, and church linen in immaculate condition. All these mundane tasks can so easily be shared, often amongst people who may not wish to take any other active part in all-age worship, and sometimes by people who seldom if ever worship in church at all, yet feel they are able to make this their offering.

Section 3. Music

From Palestrina to pop opera, pipe organ to piped bells, the role of music in the worship and ceremony of the Church is as established as it is various. The idea of interpreting man's desires and expressing his emotions through music is one that can be detected in the earliest civilisations. It is natural that Christian worship should incorporate such a means of self-expression.

What, then, are the issues to be considered with respect to the music in all-age worship? A general principle that cannot be over-emphasised is to aim for excellence. Badly-sung hymns, ragged psalm-singing, and over-ambitious voluntaries are phenomena that few of us have been able to avoid, but their effect upon the liturgy is devastating.

'We can't find choirboys and decent organists these days', grumbles the tired and disillusioned minister. If this is really the case, should not alternatives be considered rather than ploughing on with second-best? Surely, any congregation is capable of singing with enthusiasm if given the appropriate impetus. But unless the key performers are thoroughly competent, our efforts at incorporating music into all-age worship will inevitably be unsatisfactory.

If this sounds like a tall order, don't imagine that cathedral-standard organists are envisaged in every church throughout the country: far from it! Cathedral-style music would be inappropriate for the requirements of most of us. The point is simply that whatever the music you do decide to be appropriate within your own particular set-up, it should be as well executed as possible. A cathedral organist is not the only person capable of playing hymns well. He is, however, one of the few who can successfully tackle a difficult organ voluntary. So if you do not possess anyone of cathedral standard on the organ, don't aspire to have the worship cloaked in that particular style.

If an organist who can play hymns well is not to be found, there is probably someone with a good voice who could lead the congregation, possibly accompanied by guitar or other instrument. If he is good, and the context is right, the congregation will be much more inspired in their singing than if they have to compete with handfuls of unrhythmic wrong notes from the organ. And don't forget the piano; there are many more competent pianists to be found than organists. Indeed, why not explore the possibility of a church orchestra if there are local musicians about?

This leads us on to the selection of music to be made for all-age services. Obviously the choice will depend upon the resources available. Nothing should be attempted which cannot be done reasonably well, so if you do not have a good choir, don't attempt an elaborate anthem even if it does contain a point you feel to be relevant. Music should act as a catalyst in the community worship, and hymn-singing is the obvious catalyst.

In setting about the task of selecting suitable hymns, the choice of words should normally take precedence over the tunes. Remembering the large age-range present, extremes should be avoided, i.e. over-complicated words which would be difficult or even impossible for younger children and slow readers—as, for instance, 'The spacious firmament on high, with all the blue ethereal sky, and spangled heavens, a shining frame, their great original proclaim'; likewise, the 'twee' choruses written just for children need to be avoided. So when selecting the hymns, ask yourself if the words are suitable for a mature Christian to repeat. There are plenty of children's songs and choruses quite suitable for adults to sing, and there are others where you might ask the adults to sing the verse and the children to join in the chorus.

One good guideline is to look with great suspicion on any song which includes the word 'little'. Children are people; they are not 'little children' to themselves, and many of the objects we refer to in children's hearing as 'little' are not little to them: 'little birds'; 'little flowers'; 'little babies'; 'little lambs'; etc. are to small children things of normal size. For instance, the song—'Praise him, praise him, all you *little* children' should only be sung at a family service if it is altered to: 'Praise him, praise him, *all his children* praise him'. It is then made quite appropriate for everyone, as we are all 'God's children'.

If you decide to use new words in the singing, plenty of material is available, and clues as to where to hunt for it may be found in the 'Resources' section 9.

The choice of tunes is a little more difficult in that what constitutes 'good' or 'bad' music can be a never-ending debating point. Many people would dismiss 'Abide with me' as hackneyed and dreary, yet because of the broad simplicity of the tune and harmony and the fact that it matches the words, it is eminently 'singable' and therefore popular. The following points might be borne in mind:

1. We must not allow ourselves to be the slaves of our own musical preferences, but rather be sensitive to what people can obviously sing with enjoyment.

2. An attempt must be made to marry the music with the resources available. For example: 'And did those feet in ancient time' is not likely to be successfully performed when accompanied by solo guitar.

3. A fair proportion of well-known tunes should be retained when trying to introduce new music; it is very bewildering to a congregation to be presented with a barrage of unknown melodies.

4. Extremes of pitch and awkward rhythms should be avoided.

If, then, the words are appropriate, the music singable and within the scope of the congregation's ability, then the result will be a true community effort, and we shall be well on the road towards the excellence we are aiming at.

Hymn-singing is not the only form of music that is suitable to all-age worship. If you have musical talent within the church, use it as and when appropriate. If you have a good choir of the traditional variety, use them to make a particular point during the service. Once again, the age-range of the congregation should be borne in mind. So, for instance, an anthem such as Howells' 'Like as the hart' would probably appeal to most people, whereas that Palestrina motet which is a particular favourite of the choirmaster and yourself is likely to be too esoteric for the average congregation we are expecting at such a service.

Many churches do not possess choirs as such. However, solo or groups of instrumentalists can make a splendid contribution if they are not given too much to do and have plenty of time to prepare. Sometimes the leader can ask for volunteers from the congregation to form an 'instant supplementary choir', and these may include children right down to toddler age.

Such a group would stand in the midst of the people, or at the front, and the congregation should be invited to sing along with them. It is best that they should not be accompanied by the organ. A nearby piano could be used (if there is one), or they may sing unaccompanied, or alternatively accompanied by a portable instrument (guitar is undoubtedly the best, but usually needs to be amplified, especially in larger churches; flute, recorder, small drum or tambourine, or possibly a piano-accordion could also be used). Instruments such as small shakers or triangles might be given to one or two of the children. Others may be invited to join in with 'body percussion' (i.e. clapping, tapping, finger-snapping etc.).

Sometimes, recorded music or words can be used to good effect in church, but make sure that the equipment used gives a good quality reproduction.

Others may be invited to join in with 'body percussion' ...

If the family service is in the context of Holy Communion, musical settings of the Gloria, Sanctus, etc. can be used. It is important that the settings are manageable by the congregation. Palestrina was repri-manded by Pope Marcellus for writing settings that could not be under-stood by congregations, a single syllable being put to a cluster of notes, thus reducing the words' intelligibility. If for example a congregation is expected to sing the Gloria; then the music should be relatively simple and easy to learn. A gentle jazz rhythm is not out of place, as in Patrick Appleford's 'Mass of five melodies'.

The use of psalms presents a perennial problem unless your church has a good tradition of singing Anglican chants. Most churches do not have such a tradition. If it is decided that psalms are a necessary feature of the family service in a sung form, various questions need to be asked: e.g. do you wish the congregation to join in? Your church choir may be able to sing them better on its own. If it does, though, will the congregation feel alienated? If you want the congregation to join in you might try the Gelineau versions. They avoid much of the complexities of the pointing found in Anglican chant, which provides such a stumbling block for both singers and accompanist.

One of the aims in all-age worship is to involve the congregation as fully as possible, and that includes the choir. Far too often, the architecture of the building has dictated that the choir and organist should be isolated (visually and acoustically) in the chancel and may even be separated from the main body of the church by a screen. The first responsibility of a choir is to lead the congregation in the singing, and they can do this much more effectively if they are near, or preferably with the congregation.

Resiting the organist, however, is a rather bigger problem; but it is better to have the worshippers participating in the music as a whole even if it means that the organist is redundant for that particular service and the choir or instrumentalists made responsible for the leading of the music. Perhaps the organist could be asked to play a piano, or some compromise arrangement could be made after talking the matter over beforehand.

Church Song Book
There are an enormous number of Christian folk-songs and choruses available in the book-shops now. The person in charge of the music at the family service will probably have acquired a good selection of these, but on the whole it is not desirable to get the church to buy congregational copies. Practice has shown that any single collection is not adequate for all the musical requirements of family worship.

It is therefore a good idea to build up your own church song book by duplicating sufficient copies of the words for all the congregation on single sheets of A5 paper. (Of course, care must be taken to avoid infringement of copyright by seeking the necessary permission. Most publishers of material for church worship are happy to give permission for little or no fee if asked, provided the material is for use only within the church.) Then, when you have accumulated 10 to 20 different songs which you know the congregation can sing and enjoy, staple them together between some card. This system is inexpensive and has at least two other advantages:

1. you can alter the words to suit the theme or the occasion, or write in your own verses (it is as well to consult with the minister before doing this to ensure that the doctrine is sound and sensible);

2. you can select from the existing collections the songs that are most suitable, singable, and teachable. This is very important in a church where the musical resources are limited. If there is not much time for preparation, for instance, then you have to use songs or choruses that people of all ages can pick up very quickly.

It is important not to be put off in the early stages of musical experiment by apparent failures. It takes time to achieve the degree of co-operation necessary, and tensions are bound to arise to begin with, because church music is by tradition a pre-planned and often expert musical performance whereas a family service must contain a strong element of spontaneity. However, with patience, give-and-take, and a fairly frank discussion about the pros and cons, it should be possible to enlarge the scope of the church's musical offering to the great benefit of family worship in particular, and of the worship of the church in general.

Section 4. Children at the Eucharist

A point needs to be made as to the appropriateness of the Eucharist in the context of all-age worship. There is a strong body of opinion which would maintain that children should not attend a service of Holy Communion because it is something for adults, and children do not understand it.

There is good historical precedent for this idea, stemming from the ancient Church of the third and fourth centuries which reserved the sharing of the sacrament of Christ's Body and Blood for those who had been fully initiated (catechumens and others being excluded). Nevertheless, we feel justified in recommending that the Eucharist is indeed an appropriate service for all ages to attend, even if not all are allowed to receive the sacrament.

The question of understanding is not really relevant, if we mean by 'understanding' an intellectual grasp of the implications of the symbols used in worship. If we were to wait for 'understanding' of that order on the part of our worshippers before they could come to church, then worship as we know it would cease altogether, because no one would be qualified to come! How many children 'understand' in this sense the symbolic meaning of being baptised into the death of Christ, or of being joined together by God in the holy estate of matrimony? But we are happy to include them amongst the congregation at christenings and weddings without question.

To bring children to the Eucharist is an excellent means of educating them in worship, and if they respond at the altar rail with the question 'When can I have *my* drink?'—that is as good a response in its own way as that of the worshipper who devoutly makes the sign of the cross and breathes a silent prayer of thanks to the Lord.

It is common practice, where children accompany their parents to the altar-rail at the time of Communion, for the celebrant or minister to give them a blessing. If this is done, it should be a very definite action, with physical contact and with clearly enunciated words, i.e. placing your hand on the child's head and saying loudly enough for him to hear,

'The Lord Jesus bless you', 'The blessing of Christ' or some such phrase. Any indecision in this action will communicate itself to the children who will react with some puzzlement, like the two little boys whose conversation was overheard as they returned from the altar-rail:

'What did the Vicar say to you when he patted you on the head?'
'He said, "Good dog!"'

Note. Some controlled experiments are currently being tried out in the Church of England whereby children are allowed to receive the sacrament of Holy Communion at a much earlier age than the customary minimum confirmation age of 11 or 12 years. Voices are also being heard in support of a unified initiation rite such as is practised in the Orthodox churches, whereby children may be not only baptised, but also confirmed and receive the sacrament in infancy. Obviously, such thinking has a direct bearing on the question of children at the Eucharist, but at the time of writing it is not known whether it will gain currency in the Church in general, so it seems wise just to mention the fact at this stage and to reserve judgement.

It is recognised that this whole question is a sensitive area in some churches and is likely to be a matter of continuing debate. Readers who wish to go further into this question are recommended to read the following:

Children and the Sacrament of Holy Communion (available from The Methodist Publishing House, Wellington Road, Wimbledon, London SW19 8EU, 20p).

The Child in the Church (British Council of Churches 1976, 60p).

We celebrate the Eucharist, Teachers' Book, by Christiane Brusselmans (published in this country by Terry Shand and available from R.C. bookshops).

Section 5. The Art of Questioning

It is likely that more lay people will become involved in leading family services. It is also likely that one of the techniques they will employ will be to ask questions. This well-tried device for arousing and maintaining interest has, however, many pitfalls and it is hoped that the following suggestions will help inexperienced leaders to avoid potentially embarrassing situations.

Questions should be   brief
                                 direct
                                 precise
                                 simple
and   single.

Avoid such questions as 'What were we thinking about last week?'. The answers may be illuminating but not what you had in mind! In order, however, to make contact with the congregation and to establish a link with a previous family service you may want to remind them of what went on last week.

Compare the following introductions:-

(a) Q. Who remembers what Mr E. did last month?
    A. I do! *or*
       He sang in the choir *or*
       He took part in 'It's a Knockout'.

(b) Last month Mr E. showed us four pictures. Who can tell me what one of them was about? A Roman soldier. Yes, he was guarding someone. Who was the prisoner? St. Paul. What was Paul doing? Writing a letter. Yes, he was writing a letter from his prison.

(c) (Show the picture Mr E. used in the previous service.) Who is this in the picture? What is he doing? Where is he? Yes, St Paul is writing a letter from his prison . . .

From a mixed-age congregation, the youngest child or most simple-minded adult could have answered the question 'What is he doing?' Most would have known where he was, some who he was. It is important to vary the difficulty of your questions in this way and to include some for the bright, the dull and the in-betweens. Remember, though, that your purpose in questioning is to keep your listeners alert and interested: you are not trying to catch them out.

Having aroused interest, it is often possible to retain it by asking people to search for an answer in what is going to happen next. Once again, we take an example from the service which follows on from the teaching on the Epistle to Philemon referred to in Section One.

After the recollection of the epistle—
'I am now going to read you part of another letter from prison. This was written not 2,000 years ago but within my lifetime. In it the writer speaks of what makes a happy home. After I have read it I shall ask you what he considered important.'
Alternatively, another approach might be to ask the congregation to look at the picture, listen to the Bonhoeffer reading, then tell you in what way the two situations are similar.

If the main part of your presentation is to be a narrative, a safe general rule is not to break up the story by asking questions or explaining difficult concepts during the actual reading. Clear up any possible misunderstandings first: e.g. in the story of Onesimus the runaway slave, it would be best to explain first what it meant to be a slave and how difficult it was for an escaped slave to have to return to his master.

Asking the right kind of question is one desirable skill; another is that of getting answers. Have some sign such as hands up. Don't allow shouting out. Never appeal to one person openly; his mind may become a blank if confronted suddenly with the sole responsibility for answering. If a question has been planned specifically for him, watch for his hand up and then give him the chance to answer. Give time both for assimilation of the question and for thinking out the answer.

Use every answer. A wrong one may only seem so because it is not the one you expect. Take care not to discourage people by refusing a less obvious answer. Unexpected answers may be right or wrong, but an honest try must be received as such.

Sometimes there is the problem of the child who always puts up his hand and invariably gives the wrong answer, or, worse still, deliberately gives a reply with a view to causing a laugh or a disturbance. One way to avoid this trouble is to ignore this waving hand, but this is only a short-term solution.

A better way is to plan a question with this particular child in mind. If he is dull and usually gives the stock answer 'Jesus' or 'God', then ask a question to which this is the correct response. If he persists in waving his hand, it is then in order to say, 'You've had your turn, Tom. Let me hear what someone else has to tell us.' If he is exceptionally bright and is showing off, prepare a difficult question with him in mind. Take care that you have your facts straight or you may find yourself employing that escape clause dear to all school-teachers—'I am not quite sure but I will try to find out for you. You look it up as well and we will compare answers next time'.

Another useful technique is to suggest alternative answers, then ask how many people think this one is right and how many the other one. In this way all are encouraged to respond and the unwanted hand mingles with all the others.

Section 6. Different Ways of Handling a Theme

1. An address mainly for adults and brighter young people with a visual aid which will hold the attention of the others.

Speak about love and value of poetry as being a way to express our sensitivity to nature and other people. Poetry puts into words what we *feel* about things. Some of the most beautiful words in world literature are to be found in the psalms. They express the full gamut of human emotion as experienced by the Jewish people over many hundreds of years. They can be very helpful to us, and they help us to know ourselves.

Here are three verses for us to think about.

First: 'I will give thanks unto thee, for I am fearfully and wonderfully made.' (Ps.139 v 13). We see here the need for us to accept ourselves as we are. The gift of life itself is a great mystery which fills us with awe and wonder. So let us not wish to be like anyone else . . . 'I just thank you, Father, for making me *me*'.

Second: 'The Lord is my strength and my shield'. (Ps. 28. v 8). Having accepted myself, I realise how vulnerable I am. We are so often plagued by 'fightings within and fears without', and we sometimes have to face criticism from our fellows. We need the help of God to help us to develop a shield to protect us from all our enemies.

Third: 'With the help of my God I shall leap over the wall.' (Ps. 18. v 9). So we all acknowledge our need for God's protection, but we must not be content to rest there, if we wish to grow and develop as persons. We must be prepared to take risks and to leap over those barriers which we set ourselves—things we say we cannot do, either because we are afraid of being laughed at, or because we think some task is beyond us. We need with God's help to leap over the wall of our fears and limitations.

Now produce your visual aid, which will immediately draw the attention of the whole congregation—a live tortoise. Go over the points again, this time referring to Fred the tortoise. Fred accepts himself as he is, in spite of his ugliness and the heavy house on his back. Fred has a shell to act as a shield to protect him against his enemies. Fred has to 'stick his neck out'—has to take risks to get anywhere. So do we!

2. An address illustrating the technique of the non-directional approach: telling it slant. It should appeal to young people of all ages, and the others will enjoy it too. (Bible reference: Acts 9: 1–19).

The bag of bears. First produce Jonathan Bear. He is a great bear, probably bigger than many of you! The trouble with Jonathan is that he has a weight problem, and he is no good at games and P.E. He's one of those awkward bears who keeps falling over things, and dropping things, even when he is trying to be helpful.

Next, produce Golden Bear. She is a beautiful bear, but the trouble is that she knows it! She spends hours just looking in the mirror and thinking 'Ah! how lovely I am ... Aren't I lucky to have such beautiful hair and such a gorgeous complexion! No wonder all the boys just flock around me!' Of course she is conceited and proud and spoilt ... but you must admit she is cuddly!

Thirdly, produce Pooh Bear. And Pooh Bear, as everyone knows, is a bear with a very little brain. He's good at hums and he adores honey, but he's hopeless at sums and he's always bottom of the class. People call him thick and hopeless (even his teachers do sometimes), and he really thinks he is.

Finally, produce Brock-bear, a funny scruffy little bear, so called because he has a broken ear. Now this is the bear with the unknown past. (Don't tell him—but we think he came from a jumble sale!) Being a little bear he is always acting big, keeps on drawing attention to himself, and he is always in fights—hence his broken ear.

The bag of bears

Now, the sad thing about bears is that they cannot change—but the great thing about us is, that with God's help—we can!

3. An address based on pictures, with a message for older people, but younger ones will enjoy looking at the pictures too.

Select some pictures of Jesus, preferably well-known paintings from the great masters. Make sure that they emphasise quite different points. Slides are most effective. Find out a bit about the painters and the period the paintings were produced. What do they say about the different ways people have thought about Jesus?

For example:

(a) A sentimental Jesus (any nineteenth-century painting of a pre-Raphaelite kind)

(b) A powerful Jesus (El Greco's 'Cleansing of the Temple').

(c) A triumphant Jesus (A Christus Rex)

(d) Jesus as God (Renaissance painting of Jesus ruling from his cradle)

(e) Jesus as Man (Millais' painting of Jesus at the carpenter's shop)

(f) Jesus as Universal Man (Painting of Jesus as a non-European).

4. An address based on a feature of the Church building, in this instance, the bells. It should appeal to everyone.

If your church is fortunate enough to have a peal of bells, try to arrange for a set of changes to be rung before this particular service. Begin by interviewing one of the ringers to find out the general history of the tower and the bells, and the art of campanology. Then let each bell be tolled in turn a few times so that people can listen to its tone and ring. Perhaps young people in turn might be asked to do this. Then the inscription, maker and date of each bell could be spelt out. This is often very interesting. One bell made in 1700 announced: 'All you of Bath that hear me sound, Thank Lady Hopton's hundred pound'. And in 1776 on a bell in Glastonbury the founder lamented: 'Our tones would all have been much deeper if contributions had been greater'.

Then we ask what the bells teach us.

(a) They are exhilarating—they brace us for action. They cheer us up when we are gloomy and sad. They ring out joyously for nations when they celebrate victory, or for couples on their wedding day. They fill us with excitement and expectancy before worship.

(b) A peal of bells teaches us something about co-operating, working together as a team. They remind us of the discipline, both corporate and individual, we need as members of the church.

(c) We love the purity, the clarity of a bell. There are many phrases we use which reflect this idea . . . 'sound as a bell'—'true as a bell'—'it rings true'. There is something genuine about a bell as there ought to be with the true disciple. There is no hypocrisy, no dishonesty.

(d) The single 'calling' bell summons to worship almost like the voice of conscience. The person who humbly, quietly, witnesses to Christ in the ordinary humdrum things of daily life, is the sort of person which the single bell represents.

G

Section 7. The Celebrant at the Eucharist

A correspondent has written: 'Not long ago, I tuned in to a televised service from a church somewhere in the North. On the whole it was very well produced; the interviews were interesting, the hymns well sung and the church obviously cared for; but at one point the cameras closed up on the chancel where the clergy were, and they focused for a fleeting moment on the vicar. Alas! everything was wrong with him! He beat time to the music with his head, he waved his service paper up and down, and by leaning forward on his toes and back on his heels he produced a curious up-and-down movement. The result of this close-up was not only unedifying, it was outrageously funny!'

Churches do not normally have TV cameras behaving so cruelly, but nevertheless the point is made that a good many clergy have not thought out what they should be doing at the altar, liturgically speaking, when they are celebrating the Eucharist. It is obviously not possible to cover every circumstance of the eucharistic celebrant, yet we think that something should be said in view of the fact that he is such a 'key' figure and very much on show in church. The dignity and beauty of a well-ordered act of worship can so easily be spoilt by a celebrant who has no sense of the drama of the Eucharist and whose gestures are meaningless, fussy and not liturgically sound.

The following remarks are made from an Anglican point of view, assuming the rite of Series Three and presupposing a Eucharist at which the celebrant stands behind the altar, facing the people (undoubtedly the best position for family worship). The suggestions, however, should be generally helpful to celebrants who adopt other routines.

It is a valuable and rewarding exercise for any celebrant to familiarise himself with the origins of the traditional use of gesture and manual acts in the Eucharist and to teach his congregation what they mean. A useful book would be *Liturgy and Worship* by J. G. Davies (SCM 1972).

Throughout the service, the celebrant should exercise careful control over his movements, especially in the way he holds his hands. When seated, he should be sitting upright with his hands on his lap; when standing, his hands should be clasped together in front of him at waist height if they are not in the traditional attitude of prayer (i.e. palms together and fingers straight). Hands held at the side look careless and slovenly, and if they are held together loosely in front below waist level, this brings the shoulders forward and looks unsightly in any kind of vestment. To hold the hands behind the back is plainly absurd for a celebrant.

The two traditional positions of the hands in prayer are:

Position 1.   The closed position—palms together fingers extended (Fig. 1)

Position 2.   The open position—hands held about a metre apart, raised to about shoulder height, palms facing upwards and slightly inwards (Fig. 2).

The only sensible alternative to either of these positions is to clasp the hands together at waist height. In general, position 1 is used when the celebrant is doing nothing in particular, or when he is leading prayers in which the congregation join (e.g. Collect for Purity No. 4). Position 2 is used when he is praying alone on behalf of the assembled worshippers (e.g. The Thanksgiving No. 27). Position 2 is sometimes appropriately used when saying the Lord's Prayer and can be effective if a standing congregation also hold their hands in this way just for the Lord's Prayer.

The Word and the Prayers

If the celebrant is also the leader of the family service, there is likely to be an informality about the proceedings during the first part of the service. This need not be achieved at the expense of decorum, however, for the celebrant is still appointed to preside over the assembly of the people of God.

The point may be made by the way he recites the Collect, for instance, as this prayer sums up the intention of the Church for the day, and the way he says it and holds his hands (Position 2) will help to make it memorable for the people. When pronouncing the Absolution, if the sign of the cross is used, the right hand should be raised to about face height with the edge of the hand towards the people and the sign made carefully and clearly.

It is an unnecessary exaggeration to raise one's arm to its full length, and the traditional arrangement of the fingers as used by a Bishop should not be used by anyone else. These remarks also apply to making the sign of the cross at the Blessing. (Note: The first part of the blessing should be said with the hands joined, the sign being used in the second part).

If the celebrant is not officiating during the Ministry of the Word, he should be seated fairly prominently behind or in front of the altar. He may stand on occasions, but it is not normally appropriate for him to kneel (especially behind the altar where he may look ridiculous in a kneeling position).

The Offertory

The current editions of the Roman Missal talk of the offerings of the bread and wine (the oblations) being brought to the altar, and this is now very widely practised in both Roman Catholic and non-Roman churches. Representatives of the congregation should bring the gifts of bread and wine and money to the altar in such a way that they can be seen by the people. This may be done with accompanying music, but the congregation should not be singing a hymn which would prevent them from watching and sharing in the offering.

The altar vessels may be arranged on the altar before the service; the credence table should be to the *right* of the celebrant. Burse and veil, if on the altar, should be placed flat and unobtrusive. If the corporal is unfolded at the offertory, there is no need for it to be picked up as though it were a handkerchief being hung out to dry, provided that it has been properly ironed and folded in the first place. We recommend the use of a stiffened pall to cover the chalice; this will do away with the need for the celebrant to try to make a liturgical gesture out of waving away an inquisitive fly!

It is better not to have any cross or crucifix on the altar, or only a very small one which does not obstruct the people's view. It is much easier with large congregations if the altar breads are brought to the altar in a ciborium (or additional chalice) ready prepared, so that a minimum of adjustment need be made at the altar.

The server(s) should receive the oblations from the lay representatives and serve the celebrant from his (the celebrant's) right. The wine (and water) should be poured into the chalice in such a way that all can see. The celebrant may like to raise the paten and chalice slightly in a gesture of offering. If prayers are to be said, we recommend the offertory prayers from the Roman rite.

The collection of money should also be offered at this point, for it represents, together with the bread and wine, the offering of the lives of the people. The celebrant can either make the sign of the cross in blessing over the alms dish, or take it in his hands and raise it slightly in a gesture of offering. It is not necessary to lift the alms dish high in the air. The celebrant should hand the dish back to the server so as not to clutter the altar. If he is saying a prayer over the offerings, his hands should be in Position 2 (see above) and not extended over the altar. If the Lavabo (symbolic hand-washing) is used, it should be visible to the people, who should be taught what it signifies. Make sure the bowl and towel are large enough.

The Thanksgiving and Consecration
The words 'The Lord is here' do not require any accompanying gesture. (The words 'The Lord be with you', on the other hand, are a greeting and call for a gesture of greeting with the hands placed as in Position 2 but extended more towards the congregation: this would apply whenever this greeting is used, e.g. prayer no. 3.) At the words 'Lift up your hearts' the hands may be raised slightly. The basic position for The Thanksgiving is Position 2, but the hands will be joined together for the Sanctus.

The focal point of the whole of the eucharistic action is the recital of the Dominical words in the consecration. Everyone should be looking at what is happening at the altar. Provided the celebrant is taking great care both with his words and his gestures the people will see, not simply their vicar reciting a prayer, but the action of the Church fulfilling the command of her Lord. The celebrant begins the words following the Sanctus with his hands in Position 2; then, at the invocation of the Holy Spirit, they should be brought together and extended over the oblations with the palms facing downwards. This is one of the oldest liturgical gestures known to the Church and signifies the sanctifying of the bread and wine by the power of the Holy Spirit (cf. the use of this gesture by the Bishop over the candidates at confirmation).

If the celebrant wishes to make the sign of the cross over the oblations, he should do this slowly and carefully between the words 'bread and wine' and 'Body and Blood'. A single cross is sufficient here, multiple crossings being a fussy medieval practice with no liturgical significance.

In consecrating the bread, if a traditional priest's host is being used, the celebrant will simply lift it to chest height; if ordinary bread is used, it is better to take up the paten. If the celebrant bows at the Dominical words, he should do so only slightly so that his words may not be muffled. The words may be recited with a slightly lowered voice, carefully enunciated with correct emphasis. In consecrating the chalice, the same procedure is followed, with care being taken not to speak with the mouth too close to the cup as this would make the words sound hollow.

Genuflection is not an easy gesture to accomplish with dignity behind the altar. If used at all, it must be done fairly slowly with the head and back kept upright. One genuflection at the consecration will be sufficient. If the Sacrament is elevated at this stage, the host should be raised level with the forehead and the chalice likewise. If ordinary bread is used, the elevation should not take place here.

The hands are then kept in Position 2 until the Doxology. At this point, the oblations should be lifted whether or not the elevation has previously taken place. The celebrant should take the paten in his right hand and the chalice in his left, and lift them up to about chest height. (If there is a deacon present, he should lift the chalice). They are held in this way, summing up the eucharistic offering of the priest and people, until the Amen. (Note: Clergy who have been taught the old practice of continuing the service from here with the thumb and forefinger joined together should consider seriously whether this has any liturgical or practical value. It certainly looks very odd from the congregation's point of view.)

The Breaking of the Bread and the Communion
The bread must be broken so that the people can see this action. This may be the symbolic breaking of the priest's host, or the practical breaking up of ordinary bread. When ordinary bread is used, some of the difficulty experienced at the breaking may be overcome by using a large modern open ciborium. If the celebrant observes the custom of commixture (i.e. the placing of a fragment of bread in the chalice) he should do this clearly, and at some point explain the significance of it

to the congregation. The fragment must be removed unobtrusively before the general communion.

The celebrant should receive communion himself in a reverent, unhurried manner. It is appropriate for him to do so standing. A slight bow or genuflection may be made, but prolonged kneeling or, as has been seen in some churches, prostration by the celebrant is quite inelegant and distracting for the congregation and should not be done.

In administering the Holy Communion, it is better to follow the almost universal custom of starting on the south end of the rail (right-hand side looking towards the altar). If two or more people are administering, care must be taken to see that each communicant has an opportunity of a slight pause between receiving the bread and wine.

If a cloth or purificator is used to wipe the chalice, this should be done at the end of each row. To wipe the chalice between each communicant has the effect of breaking the unity we are seeking to express in the Eucharist. (Qualms about hygiene may quickly be dispelled by asking a local doctor to pronounce on the negative risk of any infection from a shared silver chalice.) To have more than one minister for the general communion is a good thing, but the practice, seen very occasionally, of one minister administering two chalices at once should never be allowed.

The Ablutions
There is no liturgical or other value in consuming the remains of the Sacrament and cleansing the vessels in front of the congregation. This is best done by an assistant on a side altar after the service. If this is not possible, it should take place during the singing of a hymn. Water alone is sufficient to cleanse the chalice; there is no need to add more wine.

At the conclusion of the service, no gesture is needed for the words 'Go forth in peace'; the hands are kept together. If the celebrant says a vestry prayer afterwards, this is for the choir and/or altar party only and should not be overheard by the congregation.[1]

Concelebration
This is when two or more priests celebrate the Eucharist simultaneously,

---

[1]A useful booklet is *The Eucharist*, Alcuin Club Manual No. 1 by Michael Perham (SPCK). For more detailed information regarding ceremonial, readers are directed to enquire about publications from The Church Union, Faith House, 7 Tufton St., London SW1P 3QN

and it may be done quite appropriately for a family Eucharist. Extra care needs to be taken with seating and grouping at the altar. The principal celebrant always presides over the assembly; the other celebrants need take no part (except perhaps in readings) until after the offertory. All the celebrants will recite the whole of the eucharistic prayer together; when the principal celebrant stretches out his hands during the invocation of the Holy Spirit and the Dominical words, the others will stretch out their right hands only over or towards the oblations.

Vesture

Introducing the Eucharist into the context of family worship (or vice versa) might be the opportunity for some churches to experiment with new styles of liturgical vesture for the celebrant. Questions of local tradition and churchmanship are often able to be set aside when bringing in a new order of service, especially if this is seen as a means of educating children and young people in worship.

There are several new patterns of liturgical vesture on the market today, and a necessary first step is to write round for brochures and price lists. The names and addresses of the leading Church suppliers are given below[1]; you should get all the brochures you can in order to compare styles and prices.

We are of the opinion that the most appropriate basic vestment for the celebrant at the Eucharist is the alb, or cassock-alb, worn with a stole of the appropriate liturgical colour. A modern chasuble is a dignified addition to this garment. It may be that, having seen the brochures, local needlewomen would like to try their hand at making vestments. This is an excellent idea, and the best way to obtain advice would be to send a notice of some kind round the diocese, possibly via the diocesan bulletin or paper, asking if any church is using home-made vestments and would share their experience of making them.

[1]Church suppliers of vestments:
Wippell Mowbray Ltd. P.O. Box 1. Cathedral Yard, Exeter. EX4 3DW.
Vanpoulles Ltd. 1 Old Lodge Lane, Purley, Surrey CR2 4DG
Louis Grossé, 36 Manchester St. London W1M 5PE
St Martin Vestments Ltd. Lutton, Spalding, Lincs. PE12 9LR

Section 8. Resources

The original plan for this section of the book was to provide useful lists of publications which we have found helpful, and to arrange them under certain classifications. With the amount of material available, however, it soon became apparent that such lists would be far too long, and would also tend to date too quickly. Instead, we shall just mention a few books and direct readers to the people and places where specialist help should be available.

RE Resource Centres have been set up in many parts of the country, some by LEAs and libraries, as well as by Churches, and we urge our readers to take the opportunity to visit them. Details of where to find them should be available at the central office of your diocese or district, or possibly from the local library, school or college.[1]

Blueprint
The most comprehensive collection of printed resource material under one cover is undoubtedly *Blueprint*. This is a series of volumes published by Galliard (Stainer and Bell) containing a vast collection of material expertly selected, arranged and catalogued. A total of 75 themes are spread over four books. Hundreds of readings and songs are printed out in full. Cross-references are made to other secular and sacred readings, songs and hymn collections. There are hundreds of reference addresses, together with notes and suggestions on classical, contemporary, folk and pop records, with details of films, filmstrips and slides. At £12.50 a volume (1979 price) this would normally be too costly for the ordinary church, but a group or Council of Churches might well invest in a shared copy.

The notes which follow are supplementary to the suggestions and ideas which appear in other parts of this book.

---

[1]A comprehensive list of RE centres has been comp. d and is available from
The York RE Centre, The College, Lord Mayor's Walk, York YO3 7EX.
It is entitled 'A Directory of R.E. Centres in England, Scotland and Wales' and is being regularly revised.
It includes information as to the kind of facilities offered by the various centres.

Prayers

Anthologies are to be found in libraries and religious bookshops; they are usually directed at one particular age-group. A good idea is to start with a collection of prayers for younger people and adapt them 'upwards', generally a more satisfactory method of approach than trying to make adult prayers easier. A useful collection is *Time and Again Prayers* (OUP). Although written for 6 to 11 years, with a little imagination it could be made suitable for all ages together—for example:

'*Road Safety:* Help me, O God, as I ride my bicycle, to love my neighbour as myself, that I may do nothing to hurt or endanger any of your children. Give to my eyes clear vision, and skill to my hands and feet, and bring me safe to my journey's end, through Jesus Christ our Lord.'

An adaptation might be:

'Help us, O God, as we ride our bicycles
                              drive our cars
                              use the roads'

or

'Help, O God, all who use the roads to love our/their neighbours as ourselves/themselves that we/they may do nothing to hurt or endanger any of your children. Give to our/their eyes clear vision, etc.'

The Lion Book of Children's Prayers (Lion Publishing) could be used in a similar way. Further anthologies which might be of help in the family service are:

Prayers for the Christian Year by William Barclay (SCM Paperback)

Prayers for Today's Church ed. Dick Williams (CPAS)—these are rather long.

Short Prayers for the Long Day, compiled by Giles and Melville Harcourt (Collins) arranged by themes and from all kinds of sources.

New Prayers for Worship by Alan Gaunt—these are presented in a folder and have supplements, such as: Supplement One – Words and Prayers for Holy Communion. (Published by John Paul, The Preacher's Press, Charlton House, Hunslet Rd. Leeds LS10 1JW).

Prayers for the Church Community compiled by Roy Chapman and Donald Hilton (NCEC).

Readings

Choosing an appropriate reading to enhance the theme of a family service can be a time-consuming task for a busy leader and one that could be delegated with good effect. Most parishes have amongst their 'human resources' the house-bound person whose mind is still active although the body is infirm. Such people could well be asked to research for poetry and prose, both biblical and secular, to fit in with the themes planned for the weeks ahead. The final choice of the material to be used could be left to the leader, but the preliminary reading would be the responsibility of the researcher.

No one book ever satisfies all needs, so it would be necessary to have several books or anthologies to hand. As the researcher may well be a retired school-teacher, it has to be pointed out that few of the books published with school assemblies in mind are of much use for all-age worship. The best of them are listed below, together with some more general anthologies. If biblical passages are chosen, the version to be used is very important. This could be another task for the researcher, who might read the different versions and then recommend a particular text for a certain occasion.

Have you ever thought . . . of using a newspaper cutting as a theme reading?

We recommend the following anthologies:

Worship and Wonder Readings and prayers chosen by Edmund Jones.

Word Alive Readings through the Christian Year, chosen by Edmund Banyard.

News Extra Readings suggested by passages in St John, chosen by Edmund Banyard.

Prophets in Action Readings suggested by Old Testament characters, chosen by Edmund Banyard.

All the above are published by Stainer and Bell.

A Book of Faith, by Elizabeth Goudge (Hodder & Stoughton). An anthology of poetry and prose arranged in themes such as Creation, God, Saints, Children, Inspiration, Faith in Old Age, Death.

Words to Share, by Donald Hilton (Denholm House Press).

Readings by Denys Thompson (Cambridge University Press)—350 passages from a wide range of sources arranged in themes. Assumes a fairly academic listener.

Assembly—Poems and Prose, by Redvers Brandling (Macmillan Education). A varied diet of literary material, 400 passages in all, divided equally between prose and poetry written by well-known, lesser-known and child contributors. Also included is a general thematic list, an appendix on hymns and records, and a valuable prose and poetry index.

Folk and Vision Book of Readings, by Hilary Elfick (Rupert Hart-Davis).
The companion volume to *Folk and Vision Book of Words and Melody*.
For Bible readings we recommend the use of *New World* (New Testament) and *Winding Quest* (Old Testament) by A. T. Dale (OUP) and also specifically for child readers *Listen!* by A. J. McCallin (Collins).

Stories and the Art of Story-telling

A good story, well told, captivates all age-groups and should therefore play an important part in family services. Listen in the first place to a recording of Johnny Morris or David Kossoff as examples of the art of story-telling at its best. It is also advisable to watch the TV programme 'Jackanory' to see how the experts do it; and we suggest you consult any local infant teachers who tell stories practically every day.

One of the best books on the subject ever written is *Stories to tell and how to tell them* by Elizabeth Clark. It was first published in 1927 and has an invaluable ten-page introduction on 'The Craft of the Story-teller'. If you cannot find a copy, ask a teacher who was trained during the 1950s, who will almost certainly have one, or speak nicely to your local children's librarian.

The diocese of Guildford has produced a training leaflet on storytelling, available from Diocesan House, Quarry St, Guildford, Surrey (5p + post.)

Collections and anthologies of stories are often produced for school assemblies but we regard them as of doubtful value for family worship. It is better to make your own collection and note down the subject, source and page under themes. The following two books may be helpful to start you off:
101 Assembly Stories, by F. Carr (Foulsham)
Steps to Glory, by Paul Chappell (The Faith Press)
We also recommend taking out a subscription to the magazine *Together*, edited by Pamela Egan (CIO Publishing, Church House, Dean's Yard, Westminster SW1P 3NZ) which often contains ideas for family services, including stories. From the same publisher come the following:
Together for Harvest
Together for Christmas
Together Again for Christmas
Together for Festivals

All are anthologies of resource ideas including plays, services and music as well as stories.

Ideas for Themes and Sermons
The most common request for help is that for new ideas. Part Four of this book contains a collection of ideas and themes which have been already tried in churches, and below you can find a list of other resource material from which further ideas can be obtained:

Celebrating Together. A resource book for Primary assemblies, by Peter Wetz and Pauline Walker (Darton, Longman and Todd). Although produced for primary teachers, this book contains themes which could be adapted, and has useful lists of addresses, ideas for drama, and sections on children's literature, Bible readings and poetry.

Many of the thematic courses produced as Sunday school material contain ideas that can be adapted for use in family services, e.g.

Alive in God's World series

Share the Word

Share the Word 2

Live, Learn and Worship, all by The Wadderton Group and published by CIO

Partners in Learning (NCEC)

In Touch—a quarterly publication for Sunday School teachers which includes material and resources for family worship. (Scripture Union, 5 Wigmore St, London W.1.)

The LEA Religious Education Syllabuses may be found to contain some useful ideas; they can be consulted in RE Resource Centres or possibly at your local school.

Ideas can also be found in the BBC schools broadcasts; you might find it convenient to tape some of their material for later use (if you reproduce it for public use, check the current regulations). Details of the schools broadcasts can be obtained direct from the BBC or possibly from your local school.

Visual and Audio-Visual Aids
To explore the possibilities in the use of these aids in family worship, your nearest RE Resource Centre would be the best place to start (see below). Two useful background books on the techniques of using AVA material are:—*Know how to use Audio and Visual Aids*, by P. W. Liddelow (Scripture Union). *Simple Techniques for Teachers* by A. R.

Nicholls (Denholm House Press). And if you want to keep up to date with the latest AVA materials for religious teaching, it is a good idea to subscribe to *AVA Magazine*, published by the British Missionary Societies and available from AVA Magazine, 17 Nether St., North Finchley, London N.12.

If you are looking for good posters and other pictures for display and/or teaching, we would recommend Argus Posters, La Rochette Pictures (Nelson), Veritas (Geoffrey Chapman), Photos Symboliques (St Paul Book Centre), Photopak (Lutterworth), and Christians Today (Kevin Mayhew). Any of the following addresses will be able to provide further details of AVA material:

Argus Communications, Plumpton House, Plumpton Rd., Hoddesdon, Herts.

St Paul Book Centre, 128 Notting Hill Gate, W11 3QG

Scripture Union AVA Dept., P.O. Box 38, Bristol

C.E.M. Publication Dept., 2 Chester House, Pages Lane, London N10 1PR

A-V for Schools, Ealing Abbey, London W5 2DY

Concord Film Council Ltd., Nacton, Ipswich, Suffolk.

Concordia Films, Viking Way, Bar Hill, Cambridge CB3 8EZ

Christian Aid AVA, P.O. Box 1, London SW1W 9BW

Church Army AVA Dept., P.O. Box 67, 185 Marylebone Rd., London NW1.

C.M.S. AVA Publications, 157 Waterloo Road, London SE1.

CPAS AV Materials, Falcon Court, 32 Fleet St., London EC4Y 1DB

The Churches' TV Centre, (cassettes and 16 mm film) Hillside, Merry Hill Rd., Bushey, Watford WD2 1DR

Religious Films Ltd., Foundation House, Walton Rd., Bushey, Watford WD2 2JF

United Bible Societies AVA Dept., 146 Queen Victoria St., London EC4V 4BX

Vigilanti AV Library, 15 Victoria Circus, Glasgow W2.

Music

It is when choosing the music for a family service that the Leader is going to become acutely aware of the generation gap, for there is now a marked difference between the repertoire of music used for church worship and that used in schools. During the past fifteen years, many schools have replaced the collections of traditional hymns which used to be their staple diet by the contemporary collections which appear in such publications as *New Life, New Orbit,* and *New Horizons* (Galliard, now published by Stainer and Bell). The BBC song book for school assemblies published in 1978 entitled *Come and Praise* contains 72 items, only a third of which would be familiar to most adults. It is therefore essential for those responsible for planning family worship to be in touch with the day school.

Day school teachers will usually be happy to share their ideas and methods with leaders of family services, and will often co-operate by teaching songs appropriate to a particular theme if given sufficient notice.

The new hymns and songs have been written to meet the demand for material to harmonise with the thematic approach to religious education which is now generally current in the school curriculum. They can therefore be very useful when family services are planned according to themes. It is suggested in the section on music (section 3) that no one book is likely to meet all the musical demands of all-age worship, and that churches should aim to build up their own collection of new hymns and songs. Out of the enormous amount of new collections, we would recommend the following titles as a basic minimum of useful books to dip into in order to provide supplementary new music for family worship:

Partners in Praise—(Stainer and Bell, 1979). This book is an obvious choice for a supplementary hymn book for all-age worship as it has been produced with the needs of the family service in mind. It includes 177 new hymns and Christian songs, some set to older tunes, which are arranged on a thematic basis. A useful feature is the cross-reference made to standard hymn-books for hymns appropriate to the various themes.

Someone's Singing, Lord (A & C Black). 59 hymns and songs, mainly new, with simple arrangements for piano and guitar and suggestions for percussion and some instrumental descants.

Sing it in the Morning (Nelson). 60 song-style hymns, mainly new yet many familiar. Clear guitar chording throughout.

Sound of Living Waters and *Fresh Sounds* (Hodder and Stoughton). 133 hymns and songs mainly new but with some established favourites; many out of the 'chorus' tradition.

New Orbit (Stainer and Bell). A feature of this collection is a section devoted to 'do-it-yourself' songs for worship.

Sing to God (Scripture Union).

100 Hymns for Today (Supplement to Hymns Ancient and Modern. (Wm Clowes & Son).

Faith, Folk and Clarity; Faith, Folk and Nativity; Faith, Folk and Festivity (all Stainer and Bell).

Come and Praise, the BBC assembly book, is available from BBC Publications, School Orders Section, 114 Bermondsey St. London SE1 3TH.

For churches who want to try the new Gelineau method of singing psalms, details can be obtained from Grail Publishing, The Grail Centre, Pemberton St., Nottingham.

The best place to enquire about musical settings of the Eucharist is The Royal School of Church Music, Addington Palace, Croydon, CR9 5AD.

(*Note*. The organ is generally an inappropriate instrument to accompany many of the new hymns and increasing use should be made of the guitar, woodwind instruments and tuned percussion. Once again, day-school music teachers may be able to help).

Drama/Dance

If there isn't a dance and/or drama specialist in the congregation, it would be advisable to make some approach either to a school or to one of the dancing schools in the vicinity if you are thinking about using these ingredients in family worship. Books on the subject are not common as it is so difficult to pass on the skills of these arts other than by personal teaching. However, Galliard (now published by Stainer and Bell) have brought out some books which suggest themes and ideas suitable for dramatic presentation:

Celebration, edited by Brian Frost and Derek Wensky. Books 1 and 2. The authors see the great occasions of the Church as an invitation to celebrate God's action in Christ by way of using a variety of different talents. The books contain suggestions for music, verbal responses, slides, subjects for debate, and the use of dance and mime as a medium for prayer.

Tension—also edited by Frost and Wensky. Books 1 and 2. This is a book of scripts which explore the creative possibilities of tension.

Let's Celebrate, by Bernard Braley. This is a book of scripts for choral speaking. They could be used simply yet effectively by inexperienced readers, or developed in the hands of an expert producer to include costume, lighting, movement and music.

You might also like to look at *Praise Him in the Dance* by Anne Long and *Time to Act* by Paul Burbridge and Murray Watts, both published by Hodder and Stoughton.

H

Section 9. Two Useful Aids

The Microphone

Churches which already have a modern amplification system will know how useful it is to reinforce the natural voice. Churches which have not so far acquired this aid, and are thinking of having family services as a regular part of the programme, should think seriously about it. It is so easy to miss vital words which can be swamped by even a very small noise in the church, and all-age worship encourages many people to speak, read lessons and say prayers who are not necessarily trained to make themselves heard in a large building. Modern column speakers direct sound so accurately that you can hear clearly without the loud-speaker seeming to be loud and without stirring up echoes. When a new installation is contemplated, the requirements of family worship should be carefully explained to the firm responsible for drawing up the specification.

Most installations provide microphones only at the front of the church, but it might be useful to think in terms of a roving microphone. If it is

Think in terms of a roving microphone . . .

thought that the trailing lead could be a drawback, investigate the possibility of a radio-microphone, checking with the Post Office to see what the current regulations are regarding their use. Alternatively, a lead from the amplifier might be taken down the church to a convenient point somewhere in the nave (perhaps along a floor heating duct) terminating in a jack point. A prayer or reading desk with a microphone attached could then be placed at this position for a particular service and then removed when it was not required.

When there is no public address system, or no chance of getting one installed, it is worth experimenting with one of the portable transistorised systems which are available. Before purchasing, one could be hired or had on approval for a few weeks to try it out. They usually consist of a short column speaker about eight inches wide and six feet high with a built-in amplifier which can be operated either by battery or from the mains. The microphone is either held in the hand, or could be on a stand or reading desk. If your local shops or firms cannot help you, write to John Catt Ltd., The Old School House, Great Glemham, Saxmundham, Suffolk IP17 2DH who could supply details of suitable firms to contact.

The Overhead Projector
Our enquiries throughout the country indicate that the overhead projector is quite clearly one of the most useful audio-visual aids suitable for family worship. It has already proved itself in industry, colleges and schools and is an excellent piece of equipment for reproducing hand-drawn diagrams, illustrations, maps, words of hymns, and summaries of teaching, the reproductions being in colour if desired. For the benefit of those not yet familar with it, here are some details.

It consists of a metal box, roughly cube-shaped, about 15 inches high containing at the bottom-centre one powerful I.Q. lamp with reflector below it and a small lens above it. The top of the box has an area cut out 10 inches square immediately below which is a Fresnel lens (a special flat lens made of plastic with concentric prisms embossed on it). Transparencies are placed on top of the box and the light shines through them from below. Then by a system of lenses and mirrors, any image on the transparency is projected over the head of the operator and on to a screen above and behind him.

The speaker, therefore, stands in front of his audience facing them in the normal way, with the projector on a table in front of him and slightly to his right (or left). When he wishes to use it he switches on, and, in a normal brightly-lit room, the pictures will appear, clear and sharp on the screen. He can point with a pencil or knitting needle to features on the transparency and the effect will be as if he were using a pointer on the screen itself. The transparency can be changed quickly, and multiple transparencies can be used, one being dropped on top of another to illustrate such topics as, for instance, the spread of Christianity across the Roman empire. The projector also has spools fitted to take rolls of the transparency material, so that the operator can simply turn a handle and the next picture moves across the screen in exactly the same way as with a film-strip.

You can draw or write freehand on the transparency, so really the projector acts as a very superior blackboard. The drawings or writing can be prepared in advance, but often the best teaching material is that which has been thought up by the speaker as he talks. Being able to display words so that everyone can read them without having to resort to large lettering is a tremendous advantage when it comes to learning new hymns, or displaying a prayer for the congregation to join in, etc.

Before investing in an overhead projector it is advisable to borrow one from a local school or college and experiment with it. The question of the screen needs careful consideration. For trials, an ordinary pro-jector screen can be used, but it is always better to have a more permanent arrangement with a correctly-angled screen to minimise distortion. Perhaps a roller-screen could be fixed to a convenient chancel screen in the church, or a hardboard screen might lie neatly away against a wall until needed, then swung out to the required position. By some means or another, the screen needs to be available speedily and without fuss and to disappear again when not in use. If a screen has to be out all the time, it should be covered in some way when not in use to remove the blank stare. To give some idea of the distance required for operation, a typical projector gives a five-foot square picture when it is eight feet from the screen.

Points to watch when buying:
Special fibre-tip pens must be used with the correct ink suitable for the acetate. These last a long time, so make sure you match up the correct pens, ink and acetate.
Ensure the picture is sharp on the screen, especially at the edges.
Check the fan noise, and the robustness of the projector, so that nothing will work loose and rattle when the fan is running.

Check whether the mirror head and arm can be detached quickly; this makes it much easier to store.

Check on bulb life and cost of new bulbs.

If the projector has to be moved around, check portability.

PART FOUR—IDEAS

Themes for All-Age Worship

Themes for All-Age Worship

In this section you will find a variety of themes and suggestions as to how they may be presented. They have all been tried out in church services during the past few years and have been well received by a variety of congregations. The section is entitled 'Ideas' because we have been so often asked by clergy and other leaders of worship where they can go to find new ideas. We are not, however, intending simply to communicate ideas in all-age worship. We are concerned to share and to explore *experience* of everyday and relate this to our understanding of God. A few of the suggestions are fairly elaborate and require a certain amount of detailed planning, possibly involving several people. Many of them, however, are relatively simple and can be prepared by a very few people (often by one person only) in quite a short time. You should glance quickly through the *Themes* and the *Aims* first of all and note down any that seem suitable. Those that are may then merit closer attention.

It should be stressed that this section is an ideas 'bank' and not a blueprint. The themes need to be used as a framework on which to build, and they will have to be adapted by the leaders to become suitable in their own local situation. They will have achieved their aim if, after some of them have been tried out, the leader is able to work out more themes of his own. In fact, material that is merely borrowed and not made one's own is never likely to be successful.

Notes. There are very few themes relating to the popular Christian festivals because so many excellent ideas appear in other publications. Reference may be made to Part 3, Section 8.

Hymnbook titles are abbreviated as follows:

Faith, Folk and Clarity	(FFC)
New Orbit	(NO)
Partners in Praise	(P in P)

Full details of hymnbooks are given in Music Section, pages 100–101.

Theme 1—Growing Children

Aim	To show the importance of unpossessive motherhood.
Occasion	Any; but particularly suitable for Mothering Sunday, Christmas 2, or festivals of the Blessed Virgin Mary.
Idea	Jesus, by what he did and said as a man, showed that he must have had good 'mothering' as a child.
Reading	Luke 2. 41–52.
Aids	Four placards (see below).
Preparation	Prepare four placards with the following words written up:

CUDDLERS	LEARNERS	EXPLORERS	LEAVERS
LOVE THEM	TEACH THEM	STIMULATE THEM	PERMIT THEM

(If used on Mothering Sunday, the words

THANK	YOU	OUR	MUM

may be written on the back.)

Music	'Lord of all hopefulness'.
	'He's got the whole world in his hands'.
	'How great the debt we owe' (P in P)

Presentation Have the placards concealed at the front. Ask the children up to 3 years old to come to the front (with mothers where necessary). Decide by question and answer that what they need most at that stage is Love. Give one of them the placard 'Cuddlers' as their label to hold up for all to see. Ask the 4 to 6 year olds to come forward. Decide (question and answer again) that these are at their learning stage. One holds the placard 'Learners' next to the 'Cuddlers'. Same routine for 7s to 9s who are the 'Explorers' and the 10s to 12s who are the 'Leavers' (partly because they leave one school for another, partly because they begin to cut loose from the family and learn for themselves).

110

Talk briefly about Jesus having passed through these stages (although we only know of stage 1 and 4 from the Gospels). His life as a grown-up shows how well he must have been 'mothered' at all stages, because:

1. he showed great love and compassion
2. he was a great teacher
3. he stimulated people with new ideas (upsetting many in the process!)
4. he allowed his disciples to fend for themselves.

(If it is Mothering Sunday, the placards can be reversed at the end of the talk for a Mothering Sunday message.)

Note. This talk involves children but will be directed more towards the adults.

Theme 2—Presents

Aim   To help people think more deeply about the meaning of gifts.

Occasion   Christmas.

Idea   Jesus is God's Christmas present to the world. He is both a 'sharing' present and a 'personal' present.

Reading   Any Christmas reading, e.g. Luke 2.

Aids   A box of Maltesers, or similar easily-eaten sweets.

Preparation It should have been announced at church or by other means that children may bring their favourite toy or gift to the Christmas family service. The leader has two 'gifts' of his own; one a personal gift, such as a fountain pen, or watch, or brooch; the other a 'sharing' present like a box of chocolates (Maltesers are best).

Music   Any Christmas music.
               'Jesus is God's gift to us' (P in P 41).
               'When the frost' (P in P 39).

Presentation Children are invited to come into the aisle and show their presents. Discussion on this should lead to consideration of two kinds of gifts: 'personal' and 'sharing'. Personal gifts are the ones you normally keep to yourself, like pens, watches, jewellery, etc. Sharing gifts are like sweets or biscuits which you normally hand round. Show your own; lead to talk about the gift of Jesus to the world. He is a 'sharing' present (the shepherds 'made known' what they had seen), and a 'personal' present (Mary pondered these things in her heart). Distribute Maltesers for good measure!

Theme 3—Assets and Liabilities

Aim   To show that, for a Christian, Christ is the most valuable asset he has.

Occasion   Re-dedication service (or any).

Idea   We must offer ourselves as we are to Christ, all that is good about us and all that is bad, for his blessing and transforming.

Reading   Philippians 3. 4–11.

Aids   Two boards covered with paper on which you may write large enough for all to see. Marking pens (black and red). One board marked 'Assets' (or 'Gains'), the other 'Liabilities' (or 'Losses').

Preparation   To save time, it may be a good idea to prepare the first 'Balance Sheet' in advance, and also possibly the third 'Assets' sheet (see below). If possible, have someone ready to give a short 'testimony' of conversion.

Music   'Take my life' (*Ancient and Modern Revised* 361).
            'In affairs of economics' (P in P 147).

Presentation The first 'Balance Sheet' is drawn up (a black marker for the Assets and red for the Liabilities) as follows:

ASSETS		LIABILITIES	
Cash in hand	£	Rent	£
Cash in bank	£	Electricity bill	£
Wages this month	£	New shoes	£
Gift expected	£	Travelling	£

Cover the first balance sheet with a second sheet of paper and draw up the second 'Balance Sheet'. This is really an up-to-date version of the 'righteousness assets' listed by St Paul in the reading: e.g.

ASSETS	LIABILITIES
Good temper	Quarrels
Charity	Meanness
Churchgoing	Laziness
Saying prayers	Complaining

Once again the items could be personal or from congregational response. Then, remembering that St Paul counted his assets as liabilities ('sheer loss', verse 8) transfer the above 'assets' to the 'liabilities' side, and introduce the third 'Assets' sheet which reads:

ASSETS
All I care for
is to know Christ.

Finish with a personal testimony of the conversion experience of coming to know Christ as the one real asset who will take us as we are, goodness and badness, and transform us into his likeness.

Theme 4—Harvest and People

Aim   To demonstrate the involvement of everybody in the harvest.

Occasion   Harvest Festival.

Idea   To offer to God, not merely thanksgiving for the gifts of harvest, but the daily work of the people in the locality, for his blessing.

113

Reading   Matthew 13. 3–9 and 18–23, or other harvest readings.

Aids   A collection of various objects depicting the life and work of local people e.g. wooden spoon (housewife); child's reading book (education); sparking plug (garage); bandage (doctor and nurse); beer bottle (leisure); weighing scales (shops and trade); file of papers (committees).

Preparation   Have the aids (above) concealed at the front ready for the talk.

Music   Harvest and thanksgiving hymns and songs.

Presentation Elicit from the congregation answers to the question—'What's going on around here?' 'What do people do in the area?' A bit of prompting with clues may be necessary; but each time there is an answer which relates to one of the objects, give the object to the person who answered and have them stand in the aisle. Having disposed of some of the objects, it will probably be necessary to reveal the rest one at a time and ask what work they relate to. Talk briefly about the harvest of daily work offered to God: then have all the people holding objects come forward and present them at the front. Sing 'All good gifts around us'—or say an offertory sentence (e.g. Series 3 Holy Communion, No. 24). This action may be combined with the Offertory or presentation of the collection and/or other harvest gifts.

Theme 5—Jesus

Aim   To discover the character of Jesus.

Occasion   Any.

Idea.   To build up a 'picture' of what kind of person Jesus was from various accounts from the Gospels.

Readings   Mt. 11.1   Mt. 15.30
             Mk. 8.1   Mk. 12.38
             Lk. 2.46   Lk. 10.21
             Jn. 19.27   Jn. 11.33

Aids	A policeman with an Identikit. The readings. Large sheet of paper and marking pen (if wanted).
Preparation	Have the readings written or typed out on separate pieces of paper. Ask the policeman to bring an Identikit.
Music	Any 'Jesus' songs e.g. from the book *Jesus Folk* by Peter D. Smith (Stainer & Bell).

Presentation 'Interview' the policeman and ask him about how an Identikit picture is made up. Possibly precede this interview (or follow it up) by standing a 'volunteer' in view of the congregation, and after he or she has sat down, ask various members what they noticed about him. (The policeman might do this for you.) Find out from the policeman how a detective discovers from clues the character of a person he has never seen.

How a detective discovers from clues the character of a person . . .

Say you want to build up an identikit of Jesus; not his looks, but what sort of person he was. Have the readings read (or re-read) as clues. They may be distributed to 8 people at the beginning of the service. Ask for suitable words to describe each clue: e.g. intelligent, teacher, etc. The words could be written up. Other readings could be used, in addition or alternatively.

Theme 6—Christians on the Move

Aim   To illustrate the Christian mission to the world.

Occasion   Any. A Missionary Sunday.

Idea   Christianity is not a static organisation, but a 'movement' (see Acts 19.2, the Way). This dynamism is exemplified by the mobility of the Apostles, especially Paul, and the work of mission today.

Reading   Extracts from Acts 18.

Aids   A globe (optional). A map (large) showing Paul's missionary journeys (which may be children's work from School or Sunday School).

Preparation 1. Write the names of the towns and countries mentioned in Acts with a marking pen on separate pieces of paper approx. 8" × 3" each. 2. Write a short letter to an ex-member of the congregation who has recently moved, or to your link missionary, to include greetings from the congregation. 3. Have the map pinned up in a prominent place in church.

Music   Hymns and songs of mission and/or pilgrimage. e.g.
               'Keep me travelling' (P in P, NO).
               'Go tell it on the mountains'.
               'All over the world'.

Presentation Before the reading, hand out the pieces of paper with the place-names on them to members of the congregation. When you introduce the reading, ask the people holding the papers to stand up when their place-name is mentioned. Begin the address with

116

a brief game of 'Stations'. Leader says: 'There is a Christian moving from Phrygia to Ephesus', and those two people change places. (Make sure no one is missed out.) Talk about Christianity as a 'movement', the work of mission, St Paul. End up by reading out the letter of greeting to the former member of the congregation or link-missionary and invite people to sign it after the service. Get someone to post it off.

The address or intercessions could include an action prayer, with members of the congregation standing round the globe and saying the following after the minister with appropriate actions:

Father of all
we lift our hands to you,
we open our arms to you,
we grasp each other's hand in fellowship.
Help us to make a circle of friendship round the globe.
for Jesus Christ's sake.   Amen.

Theme 7—Where your Treasure Is

Aim　　　　To illustrate Jesus' teaching that money is of secondary importance.

Occasion　　Any.

Idea　　　　The real treasure is God's kingdom. By following Jesus and his teaching carefully, we come to see more and more the irrelevance of money. (If this teaching is put across in all sincerity, it will benefit adults more than children.)

Reading　　Luke 12. 22.34.

Aids　　　　Record player. £1 note.

Preparation　1. Have record player ready to play 'If I were a rich man' (from 'Fiddler on the Roof') or some other song in which the singer is yearning for money. 2. Have the £1 note in your pocket.

Music　　　Hymns or songs of self-dedication; offertory hymns. 'Magic Penny'. (NO 14).

Presentation　Begin by listening to the song. Talk about dreams of becoming rich ('What would you do if you won the pools?')

117

I

Show the £1 note. It isn't money. It's a promise. Read it. It's based on faith and trust . . . etc.

Theme 8—Harvest

Aim   To bring to mind the harvest of manufactured articles.

Occasion   Harvest Festival.

Idea   God's Harvest, like man's, is a *combination* of gifts. The old idea of man's co-operation with God in providing and gathering the harvest is illustrated by reference to a *combine* harvester.

Reading   Mark 4. 3–8 and Galatians 5. 22–25.

Aids   Record player. 20 pieces of paper measuring 8″ × 3″ (you may not use them all). Marking pens.

Preparation Usual harvest preparations.

Music   At the time of writing the song 'I've got a brand-new combine harvester' by the Wurzels was popular, and appropriate to introduce the theme of the sermon. There may be other songs available which would do just as well. Other harvest music as usual.

Presentation Play the harvest song by way of introduction. Talk in general on harvest festival theme, leading to a reference to a combine harvester. Choose one or two 'scribes' from the older children. Ask the congregation what a combine harvester is made of. As each person answers, get the scribe to write the item down on one of the pieces of paper, and give the paper to the person who answered the question. Try to get the basic raw materials, e.g. wood, iron, steel, glass, plastic, rather than articles like 'seats' (countering such answers by asking 'what is the seat made of?'). When the list is reasonably complete ask the people who have got the papers to come together in the front. They then form 'a combine harvester' and (with various mimes if they wish) proceed to move slowly down the church and back again.

118

This is really just a variation on the theme of thanking God for the harvest of industry in all its variety. The system could easily be adapted to other manufactured objects.

Theme 9—St Matthew's Gospel

Aim To help people to understand something about the oral tradition and the value of learning the faith.

Occasion St Matthew's Day (Sept. 21st).

Idea Thanks for St Matthew's Gospel as the teaching document for the Church. (This is based on the assumption that it was written by a scribe for a Jewish/Christian congregation in Antioch.)

Reading Mt. 5. 1–10 or 5. 1–16.

Aids Copies of St Matthew's Gospel (TEV) which could be given away, sold or used as prizes. These can be obtained from the Bible Society.

Preparation No special preparation needed.

Music Anything appropriate to the Saints, the Bible as God's Word, or general thanksgiving.

Presentation This is a straight talk. Set the scene for the appearance of St Matthew's Gospel. Matthew, the ex-Jewish Scribe, is a leader in the Christian Church in Antioch. This Church differs little from a Jewish synagogue, and they probably keep most of the old customs. But they worship Jesus as Messiah and Lord, and hear the Jesus stories. Matthew, as a sort of schoolmaster, is concerned to teach the Jesus story to a congregation many of whom *cannot read.* They must therefore memorise. Hence the form and style of, for instance, the Sermon on the Mount. A short exercise in memory testing ('Say after me . . .') might be interesting to see how many of the congregation can learn by heart some of the Sermon on the Mount.

Theme 10—Man Does not Live by Bread Alone

Aim To show that instant solutions to problems are not necessarily the right ones.

Occasion Ash Wednesday, Lent, or Christian Aid Service.

Idea When he refused to turn stones into bread, Christ rejected the 'instant' solution to human problems in favour of the better way (God's way) of love and respect for the individual.

Reading Mt. 4. 1–4 or 1–11.

Aids A ten pence piece in a sealed envelope. A biscuit wrapped in foil. A small fishing rod (a toy or even a stick with string on the end would do)—wrapped in paper.

Preparation Have the three wrapped presents ready to give to the 'rich men' volunteers.

Music 'When I needed a neighbour'.
'Judas and Mary' (FFC).
'Savagely beat the desert sun' (P in P).

Presentation General 'background' remarks on Jesus's temptations, leading to the question 'Why didn't Jesus turn the stones into bread?' (implying that if he did, he could feed himself *and* become a popular leader by feeding others). Say you are not going to give or ask for an answer, but tell a Chinese story.

Have three 'volunteers' to represent three poor people who live by the sea. Talk with them about the meaning of poverty (no money, food etc.). Have three more volunteers to be three rich people who give them presents. First present is money: second is a biscuit: third is a fishing rod. The 'poor' unwrap their presents, one at a time. Discuss with the recipients and/or congregation who has the best present, leading to the conclusion that the fishing rod is the most sensible gift. Why?

Theme 11—Sunday is not Sabbath

Aim To show why Jesus broke the Sabbath rules.

Occasion Any.

Idea	To contrast Jewish (and Puritan) Sabbath with the Christian Sunday: thereby contrasting pharisaism with the love and compassion of God in Christ.
Reading	Luke 6. 1–11.
Aids	Plain bandage and bandage with medication.
Preparation	None.
Music	'This is the day that the Lord has made' (P in P). 'The day of Resurrection'.
Presentation	Initiate discussion (or question and answer) on 'things we can do on Sunday'. Volunteers might mime some of

the things for the congregation to guess. (If they can't supply their own ideas, suggest: driving car, washing up, cooking dinner, gardening, going for a walk, bike ride.) Ask older members of congregation what they used to do on Sunday, and couldn't do. Supply information about old Jewish Sabbath . . . . no work: but what is work?—cooking, carrying burdens, walking. And also *no healing,* except emergency: e.g. plain bandage could be applied, but not a medicated one. So, the disciples in the cornfields were breaking four rules(i.e. reaping, threshing, winnowing, and preparing a meal.) And Jesus broke another one by healing. Develop into Jesus's demonstrating the 'rule of the love of God'.

Theme 12—Family at Worship

Aim	To show the value of family prayers in church or at home.
Occasion	Any.
Idea	Christian family worship is based on Jewish forms, but differs from them in many respects.
Reading	A Bible reading is not essential but part of the Last Supper account could be used, or I Cor. 11. 23–26.
Aids	The 'Schema' and the Jewish Mother's Family Prayer for the Sabbath written out (see below). Candle (lit or ready to light). Cup. Bread roll.

Preparation   Write or type out the 'Schema' as follows: 'Hear, O Israel, the Lord our God is One. And thou shalt love the Lord thy God with all thy heart, with all thy soul, and with all thy might. 'And also the Jewish Mother's Prayer as follows: 'Father of mercy, continue your loving-kindness to me and to my dear ones. Make me worthy to bring up my children so that they will walk in goodness before you, loyal to your law, and always busy in good deeds. Keep us from all shame, grief and care; grant that peace, light and joy may always abide in our home. Because you are the fountain of light, and in your light we see light. Amen'.

Music   'Let us break bread together'.
'Kum ba ya.'

Presentation   'Borrow' a family from the congregation, consisting if possible of father, mother, and two or three children. Give mother the Jewish Mother's Prayer, and father the Schema. Have a candle ready to light nearby (or lit). Explain how Jews have their family worship at home on Friday evening at 6 pm. The mother (Mary, perhaps) lights the Sabbath candle (action), and reads the Jewish Mother's Prayer (she reads it). The shared cup is passed round as a sign of unity (action, possibly) and then a piece of bread is broken and shared as a 'grace' (action, possibly). The meal follows, and afterwards the father (Joseph, perhaps) reads the 'Schema' (he reads it), and tells Bible stories.

Follow this with a brief description of the Saturday synagogue worship. Compare with Mattins or other non-eucharistic Christian worship. Contrast 'men only' worship with modern Christian family worship.

Theme 13—The Lights of Christmas

Aim   To explore another angle to the Christmas story.

Idea   The two lights of Christmas lead to the third 'holy' light of the manger.

Reading   Any nativity reading

Aids   Lantern (lightable); taper; matches; candles; cardboard star; low stool or chair; doll.

122

Preparation Make sure the lantern can be lit. The star can be of cardboard with silver foil; it should be big enough to be seen easily by the congregation. The doll may be swaddled but this is not essential.

Music Any Christmas music.

Presentation Hold up a paraffin lantern for all to see. Ask a boy to hold it for you; light it (with taper). Talk about Christmas lights. Ask how many there are. In fact, there are only two biblical lights; the angels and the star, but others may be forthcoming, e.g. candles or fairy lights on the Christmas tree, lantern in the stable, etc.

Use those who give answers to form a group in the centre or at the front; one to hold the star, others to hold candles. Talk of the two Christmas lights ... guiding light (star) and warning or announcing light (glory of angels). Lead up to talking about a third light—the 'Holy Light' of Jesus which gave a special glow to the stable (cf. story of the light in Mother Teresa's Home for Derelicts; see *Something Beautiful for God* by Malcolm Muggeridge, (Fontana) (page 44) The group holding lights could become an instant Nativity tableau—choose a Mary and give her the doll and a seat. Let the lantern-bearer become Joseph, and the rest shepherds, kings or angels.

Theme 14—Christian Preparedness

Aim To show that to be Christian is to be ready for God.

Occasion Annunciation. Advent.

Idea Mary's 'preparedness' to become the mother of Jesus is compared to the idea of Christian readiness (the Advent theme).

Reading Lk. 1. 26–30 and 38 (could be dramatic reading).

Aids None.

Preparation None.

Music	Advent music. Annunciation hymns or songs.
	'Long ago prophets knew' (P in P).
	'When he comes back' (*Hymns and Songs*.
	Methodist Publishing House.)

Presentation Ask for the co-operation of the ladies in the congregation.
A specified number (say eight) will be asked to produce one item each from their handbag. Select eight children to collect these items. The children stand in centre of front to show what they have got. (If there are too many 'repeats', arrange some swops). Ask the ladies why they have got these items in the bags, and try to lead the conversation round to 'preparedness'. (Refer if you like to the Scout/Guide motto and produce the standard equipment which every good Scout is supposed to have on him: money, pocket knife, notebook, and pencil, etc.)

Now ask for help from mothers and obtain a list (verbal or written) of items needed in preparation for the arrival of a new baby. Link up the two ideas of preparedness i.e. (a) ready for anything and (b) ready for a special event. Explain how Mary was ready for the coming of Jesus because she was *always ready* for God to speak to her in prayer. That is why she was chosen to be the Mother of the Lord.

Theme 15—The Church—What and Why

Aim	To answer the question—'What is the Church?'
Occasion	Any. Last Sunday before Advent.
Idea	The Church is a mixture of all kinds of people, meeting for a common purpose, prayer and worship and to offer themselves for God's blessing.
Reading	1 Cor. 12. 12 and 14–20, and 27.
Aids	Sufficient pieces of paper 8" × 3" for the whole congregation. Pencils, large pudding bowl, wooden spoon, Parish Prayer list.
Preparation	Have the Prayer List duplicated. It could be a simple street prayer scheme, whereby different streets are prayed for each day of the month.

| *Music* | Hymns or songs relating to the Church and/or prayer, e.g. 'O worship the Lord in the beauty of holiness'; 'God is here, as we his people' (P in P). 'Church metaphors.' (P in P). |

| *Presentation* | Have some volunteer children to give out the pieces of paper and pencils to congregation. Ask the congregation |

to write down what they do for a living (children, what they want to be when they grow up; retired, what they used to do). Collect the papers in the bowl (it may be as well to assure the congregation that nobody will read the papers except yourself as some people may be sensitive about handwriting or spelling). Talk about the Church as a mixture of all kinds of people ... select a few of the occupations to illustrate the point. If it is the Sunday before Advent, you may like to 'stir' the papers with spoon! The bowl can be placed on the altar as a symbolic offering of ourselves for God's blessing. Give out the Parish Prayer Lists to be used during the coming week, month, year ... as an example of what the Church does for the local community.

Theme 16—Learning to Love

| *Aim* | To show the importance of family life. |

| *Occasion* | Any. |

| *Idea* | The family is the context in which human beings learn to love. It is by learning to love within the family that we |

are enabled to live loving lives outside it and this process takes time.

| *Reading* | Lk.2. 41–52 or 1 John 4. 7–12 or Mt. 25. 31-end (extracts) according to teaching emphasis. |

| *Aids* | A baby animal; a human baby. Or large pictures of these. |

| *Preparation* | It may be advisable to warn the mother with the baby and ask for her help before the service. If a baby animal |

is used, make sure it can be stowed away after it has been shown so that it doesn't become a distraction during the rest of the service. Pictures are safer, but less exciting; they should be large. (A professional photographer will probably loan or give these if asked.)

Music   'Bread is the laughter' (NO 37).

Presentation   Contrast the time it takes for a young animal (show it, or picture) and a young human (ditto) to leave home. Then, via question and answer, move towards the question 'Why do human beings take so long to grow up?' ... and the answer: because God gives them time to learn to love, according to his will and loving purpose for his children. The family, therefore, is the place where human beings, parents as well as children, are learning this great lesson of love. To link this with the reading from Matthew's Gospel, reference could be made to the caring for children who have no family of their own ... Children's Society, fostering, adoption etc.

Time for a young animal and a young human to leave home ...

Theme 17—Growing up with the Bible

Aim   To show how the Bible speaks to us all through our life.

Occasion   Any. Bible Sunday.

Idea   Scripture is important to us at every stage of life. This might be demonstrated from any suitable and familiar biblical passage; here we use Psalm 23.

Reading   Could be Psalm 23; or if this is sung, another suitable story which would allow of similar treatment and to which brief cross-reference may be made, e.g. Jairus' daughter (Lk.8.41); Feeding of 5000 (Jn.6.1. ff); Hymn to Love (1 Cor. 13.1 ff).

Aids   Large pictures, or objects, or placards representing the 'Five ages of Man' (see below). Copies of Ps. 23 available to congregation.

Preparation   Have ready to be displayed objects to illustrate the 'Five ages of Man' Baby, Junior, Teenage, Adult, Old-age, e.g. bottle: football: lipstick: electricity bill: walking stick. Or five pictures— or five placards with the words 'Baby' etc. written on. Make sure the congregation can see a copy of Psalm 23.

Music   Any setting of Psalm 23.

Presentation   Refer to the 'Five ages of Man' (reduced from Shakespeare's seven ages in *'As You Like It')*. Use the prepared display material during the talk in some appropriate way as visual aid, perhaps with five volunteers.

The Bible is a 'book for life'. Many of its stories and writings have something to say to each stage of living. For instance, Psalm 23:

Baby: The infant's prime need is for *nourishment* with *love*. 'The Lord is my Shepherd . . . he shall *feed* me.'

Junior: This is the age to sort out right from wrong. The age for getting into scrapes. 'He shall bring me into the paths of *righteousness.'*

Teenage: The age for finding out who really are your friends: importance of *relationships*. In Psalm 23, in verses 1 to 3 the writer addresses God as 'He' (third person). From v. 3 onwards, God is addressed in the second person; You, Thou. And when you have found your friends, true fellowship begins, symbolised perhaps by a *shared meal:* 'Thou hast prepared a *table'.*

Adult: The 'busyness' of adult life. Home, family, job. This means (1) increase of tension and anxiety; need for inner healing. 'Thou hast anointed my head with *oil'*. And (2) less time for reflection or prayer; God may be left behind, or forgotten. But God never forgets you. 'Thy loving-kindness and mercy shall follow me all the days of my life.'

Old age: Approaching the unknown. 'The valley of the shadow'. But 'thou art with me; thy rod and thy staff comfort me'.

Theme 18—Good News

Aim   To present the Bible as Good News.

Occasion   Any. Bible Sunday.

Idea   'The News' on the media is so often bad. The Bible contains good news for the faithful, and that is what 'Gospel' means.

Reading   Short extracts taken almost at random from any part of the Bible should be included in the address. e.g. Gen.1.1–3: Ps.121. 7 and 8: Mk. 9.13: Lk.2.8.ff: Lk.8.54: Jn.20.19: Acts 3.5 ff. If a separate Bible-reading is wanted, any Bible story which can be classed as 'good news' may be read.

Aids   A Bible. The letters G-O-D-S-P-E-L on separate cards large enough for people to see when held up at the front.

Preparation Have the short extracts ready to hand to be read, either marked in a Bible or typed out and distributed for various people to read. Six extracts will be sufficient. Have the GODSPEL letters ready to be held up at the front.

Music   'Lord of the dance'.
               'We have a Gospel to proclaim'.
               'God's spirit is in my heart'.

Presentation Start by asking for recent news items. See how they are often bad news. Draw attention to the Bible as good news. Read (or have read) the extracts. Comment briefly on them if necessary. Select 7 volunteers to hold up at the front the letters G-O-D-S-P-E-L. Point out how 'SPEL' is the Anglo-Saxon word meaning 'news', and 'God' is the Anglo-Saxon word meaning 'good'. Ask which letter should be removed to make a familiar Bible word.

Theme 19—Donkey

Aim   To suggest that the choice of you as a disciple might be a risk for Jesus.

Occasion	Palm Sunday
Idea	Jesus took a risk in choosing a donkey as a mount: he might be choosing you today to carry him in the world.
Reading	Matthew 21. 1–11
Aids	A ball (tennis ball would do).
Preparation	None.
Music	Any for Palm Sunday. 'We have a king who rides a donkey' is suitable for younger children.

Presentation   Have a few volunteers to play 'Donkey' (i.e. throw the ball to one another. The 1st time you drop it you are a 'D' ... the 2nd time you are a 'DO' ... the 3rd time a 'DON' ... and so on. The first person to drop it 6 times is a 'Donkey' and has to leave the game). The game will probably have to be adjusted according to time available.

We don't like to be called a 'donkey'—why? Discuss the characteristics of a donkey ... slow and stubborn and they bray. We can be donkey-minded when we want our own way, and it must sound like braying in God's ears when we complain, or are malicious or unkind. Yet Jesus *chose* a donkey. It was a risk. He might be choosing you to carry him today.

Theme 20—Coronation of Jesus

Aim	To teach about the Ascension.
Occasion	Ascensiontide.
Idea	The Ascension of Jesus is really the culmination of a process. His life and works are, in effect, a continual ascension.

Reading	Mt. 28. 16–20 or Acts 1. 6–11.

Aids Seven legible placards with the following words written on them: Baptism: Temptation: Healing and Teaching: Suffering: Dying: Living again: Crowning. You also need a crown (made of card and covered with foil) on a cushion.

Preparation See Aids. A chair should be placed front/centre and preferably raised.

Music Any hymns or songs for the Ascension. A recorded fanfare could be used if desired.

Presentation The floor-level of the medieval Church of St Mary, Temple Balsall, (near Birmingham), rises in seven steps from the West door to the altar. These steps are said to correspond to the seven orders of knighthood of the Knights Templar who used this church. So each knight had his place according to rank, from the young squire near the door, ascending to the fully-fledged knight near the altar.

Use this as an introduction to thinking of Christ as the perfect example of chivalry, and by talk or question and answer, trace his 'Ascension' from his Baptism to his Crowning (the Ascension proper) as follows:
1. Baptism 2. Temptation 3. Healing and Teaching 4. Suffering. 5. Dying. 6. Living again. 7. Crowning.

Eight volunteers are needed. Nos. 1 to 6 can stand in order from the back to the front of the Church and can be given the cards as the answers arrive (or at the appropriate time in the talk). No. 7 (Jesus) will then walk from the back to the chair at the front/centre and sit down; No. 8 will follow and give him his card (and place the crown on his head if a crown is being used). This presentation is not intended as a piece of drama; it can be done without rehearsal and the preacher should stage the whole thing while he is talking.

THE OFFCHURCH GROUP

John Hall-Matthews is the Vicar of St Paul's Church, Tupsley, in the diocese of Hereford. Before his appointment in 1975 he was for ten years school chaplain at Christ's Hospital, Horsham in Sussex, and at the Royal Hospital School at Holbrook, near Ipswich, Suffolk. His present appointment keeps him in close contact with two large comprehensive schools and a primary school. He is married to a doctor and has four children.

Brian Hardy is chaplain of the Scottish Episcopal Church's theological college in Edinburgh. The greater part of his ministry has been spent in new communities, including new town work in England and Scotland. He is deeply interested in ecumenical ministry, ordained and 'lay', as well as in music.

Kathleen Hovey is a primary school teacher in a semi-urban village in Cheshire. For many years she has been concerned with voluntary religious education in the diocese of Chester at parish, deanery and diocesan level. She is married and has two teenage sons.

Martin Tunnicliffe is Vicar of Tanworth-in-Arden in the diocese of Birmingham. He has been in the parochial ministry in the Birmingham diocese since 1960 and has served in both town and country parishes. He has a particular interest in the Church's work with children and was a member of the Children's Publications Group of the General Synod Board of Education from 1976 to 1979. He is married and has three children.

ACKNOWLEDGEMENTS

This book would never have been completed without a good deal of expert help which the writers were able to draw on. In particular, the writers would like to acknowledge the assistance of Peter Smith, Bernard Brayley and Carl Attwood who have helped with the music sections, Alan Beck who provided material on audio-visual aids, and Barry Miller who assisted as consultant in the early stages. We are grateful to Philip Jones and John Mortiboys who provided material for the section on the Celebrant at the Eucharist, and to David Tennant for reading and commenting on the manuscript from the Free Church point of view. We owe a debt of gratitude to Kevin Butcher for his inspired drawings, to our various anonymous typists who have assisted in the preparation of the manuscripts and to a number of correspondents who have kindly written to us about their family services. We should like to record our thanks to the Bishop of Coventry for writing the Preface, and to those kind folk who read the book in manuscript and made many helpful comments and suggestions, as well as to Pamela Egan for shepherding the book and its writers through the various tortuous stages of its pre-publishing existence. Last but by no means least, the Offchurch Group takes its name from having met in conference on various occasions at the Coventry Diocesan Retreat House at Offchurch, and therefore we wish to express our thanks to Arthur and Rosemary Russell, the wardens of the house, who kindly saw to our material needs and comforts while we were there.